Coretta
Scott King

Other books in the People in the News series:

Al Gore
David Beckham
Beyoncé
Fidel Castro
Kelly Clarkson
Hillary Clinton
Hilary Duff
Dale Earnhardt Jr.
Zac Efron
50 Cent
Tony Hawk
Salma Hayek
LeBron James
Angelina Jolie
Ashton Kutcher
Tobey Maguire
John McCain
Barack Obama
Nancy Pelosi
Queen Latifah
Condoleezza Rice
J.K. Rowling
Shakira
Tupac Shakur
Ben Stiller
Hilary Swank
Justin Timberlake
Usher

Coretta Scott King

by Anne Wallace Sharp

LUCENT BOOKS
A part of Gale, Cengage Learning

GALE
CENGAGE Learning

Detroit • New York • San Francisco • New Haven, Conn • Waterville, Maine • London

LIBRARY OF CONGRESS CATALOGING-IN-PUBLICATION DATA

Sharp, Anne Wallace.
  Coretta Scott King / by Anne Wallace Sharp.
    p. cm. – (People in the news)
  Includes bibliographical references and index.
  ISBN 978-1-4205-0087-5 (hardcover)
  1. King, Coretta Scott, 1927-2006–Juvenile literature. 2. African American women civil rights workers–Biography–Juvenile literature. 3. Civil rights workers–United States– Biography–Juvenile literature. 4. African American women–Biography–Juvenile literature. 5. African Americans–Biography–Juvenile literature. 6. King, Martin Luther, Jr., 1929-1968–Juvenile literature. 7. African Americans–Civil rights– History–20th century–Juvenile literature. 8. Civil rights movements–United States– History–20th century–Juvenile literature. I. Title.
  E185.97.K47S54 2009
  323.092–dc22
  [B]
                                                                              2008029894

Lucent Books
27500 Drake Rd
Farmington Hills MI 48331

ISBN-13: 978-1-4205-0087-5
ISBN-10: 1-4205-0087-2

Printed in the United States of America
2 3 4 5 6 7 12 11 10 09

Contents

Foreword

Fame and celebrity are alluring. People are drawn to those who walk in fame's spotlight, whether they are known for great accomplishments or for notorious deeds. The lives of the famous pique public interest and attract attention, perhaps because their experiences seem in some ways so different from, yet in other ways so similar to, our own.

Newspapers, magazines, and television regularly capitalize on this fascination with celebrity by running profiles of famous people. For example, television programs such as *Entertainment Tonight* devote all of their programming to stories about entertainment and entertainers. Magazines such as *People* fill their pages with stories of the private lives of famous people. Even newspapers, newsmagazines, and television news frequently delve into the lives of well-known personalities. Despite the number of articles and programs, few provide more than a superficial glimpse at their subjects.

Lucent's People in the News series offers young readers a deeper look into the lives of today's newsmakers, the influences that have shaped them, and the impact they have had in their fields of endeavor and on other people's lives. The subjects of the series hail from many disciplines and walks of life. They include authors, musicians, athletes, political leaders, entertainers, entrepreneurs, and others who have made a mark on modern life and who, in many cases, will continue to do so for years to come.

These biographies are more than factual chronicles. Each book emphasizes the contributions, accomplishments, or deeds that have brought fame or notoriety to the individual and shows how that person has influenced modern life. Authors portray their subjects in a realistic, unsentimental light. For example, Bill Gates—the cofounder and chief executive officer of the software giant Microsoft—has been instrumental in making personal computers the most vital tool of the modern age. Few dispute his business savvy, his perseverance, or his technical expertise, yet critics say he is ruthless in his dealings with competitors and driven more by his desire to maintain Microsoft's dominance in the computer industry than by an interest in furthering technology.

In these books, young readers will encounter inspiring stories about real people who achieved success despite enormous obstacles. Oprah Winfrey—the most powerful, most watched, and wealthiest woman on television today—spent the first six years of her life in the care of her grandparents while her unwed mother sought work and a better life elsewhere. Her adolescence was colored by promiscuity, pregnancy at age fourteen, rape, and sexual abuse.

Each author documents and supports his or her work with an array of primary and secondary source quotations taken from diaries, letters, speeches, and interviews. All quotes are footnoted to show readers exactly how and where biographers derive their information and provide guidance for further research. The quotations enliven the text by giving readers eyewitness views of the life and accomplishments of each person covered in the People in the News series.

In addition, each book in the series includes photographs, annotated bibliographies, timelines, and comprehensive indexes. For both the casual reader and the student researcher, the People in the News series offers insight into the lives of today's newsmakers—people who shape the way we live, work, and play in the modern age.

The First Lady of the Civil Rights Movement

C oretta Scott King was a witness to and a participant in some of the most momentous historic events of the twentieth century. She stood side by side with her husband, Martin Luther King Jr., during the civil rights movement that swept the United States in the 1950s and 1960s. She saw the passage of the Civil Rights Act of 1964 that mandated equal rights for all Americans regardless of race, and also saw the end of school segregation in the South.

Following her husband's assassination in 1968, King continued to fight for equality for African Americans. She also witnessed and participated in the ending of apartheid, a severe system of discrimination against blacks, in South Africa. She fought for gay rights, women's rights, and an end to the nuclear arms race. She sought support for and then witnessed the first national holiday to celebrate an African American—Martin Luther King Day. And finally, in building the King Center in Atlanta, Georgia, she created a place where her husband's life and dreams are honored and his theories on nonviolence are taught to thousands of young activists.

Growing up in the segregated South, King experienced racism at its worst and rose above it. She began speaking out against discrimination at Antioch University in Ohio while still in her early twenties. She often credited her parents and her childhood for giving her the determination to lead a life dedicated to helping her fellow African Americans overcome racism. Marian Wright Edelman, a longtime friend of King and the founder of the Children's Defense Fund summarizes: "Coretta King said that even as a child, she felt she was going to lead an extraordinary life. Many people might not have expected that from a little Black girl who grew up in very rural Alabama during the Depression, picking cotton, and walking several miles each way every day to attend a segregated one-room school. But from the start, she was exceptional."[1]

Pursuing a musical career, King excelled at college and dreamed of becoming a concert singer. She gave up that dream to follow another one as the wife of charismatic minister and activist Martin

Coretta Scott King smiles before a backdrop image of her late husband, civil rights leader Martin Luther King Jr., at the King Center for Nonviolent Social Change in Atlanta, Georgia, in 2004. Coretta created a legacy of her own through her work on a range of social justice issues beyond those advocated by her husband, including gay rights, women's rights, and anti-war activism.

Luther King Jr. During the tumultuous times of the 1950s and 1960s, she stood firmly behind her husband and faced the hatred that was directed at them with courage and dignity. Following King Jr.'s assassination, she not only raised four remarkable children but also tirelessly carried on the fight for equality. She never shied away from a struggle for the things she believed in, and she spoke on behalf of many issues that others chose to ignore. Brian Robinson of *ABC News* said: "She will be remembered as an activist who not only carried on her husband's legacy but forged her own legacy of peace, tolerance, and understanding."[2]

Often called the First Lady of the civil rights movement, King was more than just Martin Luther King Jr.'s wife. She was, in fact, a full participant in the movement toward equality for African Americans. Journalist Ernie Suggs elaborates: "It would have been easy to label Coretta Scott King just a wife, but it would have missed the mark. Before she married . . . Coretta Scott had established herself as a politically and socially conscious young woman. . . . She was an anti-war activist who rallied fellow students against violence. . . . She [later] became an international advocate for peace and human rights. She met with presidents and world leaders . . . and well into her 70s, she traveled the globe to speak against racial and economic injustice, promote the rights of the powerless and poor, and advocate religious freedom, full employment, health care, educational opportunities, nuclear disarmament, and AIDs awareness."[3]

After King's death from cancer in January 2006, many U.S. politicians and leaders gathered to praise and honor her. Reverend Al Sharpton spoke of her activism: "She was a real activist. She had one of the most keen, aggressive social, political minds that I have ever talked to. She was really committed to world peace, really committed to racial equality, really committed to civil disobedience, and nonviolence. She was not just the woman he [Martin Luther King Jr.] went home to. She was the one who shaped his ideas and activism and she singled-handedly maintained his legacy."[4]

President George W. Bush spoke for many Americans when he summarized King's extraordinary life: "In all her years, Coretta Scott King showed that a person of conviction and strength could also be a beautiful soul. This kind and gentle woman became one of the most admired Americans of our time. She is rightly mourned and she is deeply missed."[5]

Coretta Scott King earned her place in history through her hard work and support of her husband. Following his death, rather than remaining silent and retiring from public life, she continued the fight for equal rights for all Americans—and for all people. As President Bush said, she will be deeply missed.

Chapter 1

Growing Up with Segregation

Coretta Scott King grew up in the midst of the Great Depression of the 1920s and 1930s. This was a hard time for everyone, but particularly for Southern blacks because of high unemployment and extreme poverty. King, however, was luckier than many other African American children in that her father owned a farm that enabled her family to put food on the table even during the worst of times.

King also grew up during one of the harshest times in American history for African Americans. It was a time of discrimination and heightened racism that lasted from the late 19th century to the mid-1950s. Blacks were forbidden by law to eat, sit, go to school, or have any kind of social contact with whites. African Americans were frequently victims of violence, ranging from harassment to lynching.

King describes the era: "They [white Southern governments] made it illegal for Blacks and Whites to eat together in public; to sit together in theaters, buses, or trains; to use the same comfort stations or water fountains; even to enter public buildings by the same door. It was as though Blacks had some contagious disease . . . the whole idea was to impress upon the Black people that we were an inferior race."[6]

An Impressive Family

Coretta Scott King was born at home on April 27, 1927, in Marion, Alabama. Her father Obadiah Scott farmed his own land, while her mother Bernice McMurry Scott helped with the farm and raised three children. King was the youngest of three children; her siblings were sister Edythe and brother Obadiah. She was named after her grandmother Cora, a woman of spirit and strength who had helped sustain her own family during hard times.

Coretta's extended family had long been leaders of the rural black community. Her paternal grandfather, Jeff Scott, was an important man in the area and was always referred to as "Mr. Scott." He owned a 300-acre (121ha) farm and was a church leader. His wife, Cora, who died before King's birth, was known for her strength and drive. King's maternal grandfather, Martin McMurry, taught himself to read the Bible and was still walking the 12 miles (19km) to town and back when he was seventy years old. Both men were active in both community and church affairs.

A young boy in North Carolina during the 1930s stands at a drinking fountain identified for use by "colored" people only, as dictated by Jim Crow laws. When Coretta was growing up, she experienced similar indignities of segregation and harassment that oppressed the rights of African Americans in the Depression-era South on a daily basis.

Coretta's parents were also remarkable people. Years later in an interview with Vern E. Smith, King recalled her parents: "I had great parents. My father was one of the strongest men, emotionally and physically. He never became bitter though he had been persecuted trying to feed his family. My mother was also very strong, a feminist for her time. She did things that men did, and later drove a school bus."[7] At that time school buses were typically driven by men and King's mother was one of the first women school-bus drivers. This placed her in danger of being abused by the area's white population. King's father was the first black man in the county to own a truck, which he used to supplement his farm income by hauling logs for the local sawmill. Journalist Vicki Crawford elaborates: "The Scotts embraced the values of faith, hard work, service, leadership, and integrity and passed these along to their three children."[8]

The Scotts lived in a modest two-room house containing two double beds, a dresser, and an open fireplace. Coretta and her siblings slept in one bed while her parents slept in the other. Water for the home came from a backyard well. One of their most prized possessions, according to King, was a Victrola, one of the earliest kinds of record players. Coretta remembers, "We had an unusual collection of records. I remember such treasures as Clara and Bessie Smith recordings, sermons, and jazz recordings, as well as popular songs and hymns."[9] She spent long hours listening to the music and singing along. When not listening to music, Coretta played outside with her siblings and numerous cousins. She wore her hair in braids and was somewhat of a tomboy, climbing trees and wrestling with friends. She did not like being teased and had a fiery temper.

All of the children learned to work early in life to help the family survive. Coretta, for instance, was six or seven when she started working in the fields of her parents' farm. The Scotts grew corn, peas, potatoes, and other vegetables. They did not sell their crops. They used them for meals and for food for their animals, primarily hogs, chickens, and cows. Coretta also helped milk the cows, feed the pigs, and gather eggs. With everyone in the family helping, the farm provided enough food to keep the family well fed and self-sufficient during the worst years of the Depression.

Although they were usually small, modest structures, African American churches in the Depression-era South, such as this one in Louisiana, were the center of their members' social lives. The Scott family was active in their own church, where Coretta developed her interest in music.

Church

For the Scotts, like thousands of other African American families, their church was the center of their social life. They attended Mount Taber AME Zion Church. The church was 4 miles (6.4km) from their home so the entire family walked to and from church services on Sunday. The church itself was an unpainted wooden building heated by a pot-bellied stove; light was provided by kerosene lamps.

Due to the lack of black ministers in the South, Mount Taber only had an official church session every other week. On the other Sundays, the children and adults attended Sunday school and had a brief prayer service, usually led by Coretta's grandfather, Jeff Scott. Unlike black ministers of the 1950s and 1960s, black church leaders in the 1930s and 1940s seldom addressed the racial issues of their day. It was simply too dangerous to even discuss the rights of blacks, much less take action.

Each month there was a children's day at Mount Taber during which the youngsters presented a program of songs. Coretta sang solo on many occasions, and by the time she was fifteen, she had become the church's choir director and pianist. She trained dozens of young people and also wrote several musical programs that were presented to the congregation. Coretta, repeatedly over the years, credited her church activities with helping her develop her strong interest in singing and music.

Coretta later described the importance of church in her young life: "To me, as a child, church was a warm and heartening experience; with . . . all my family there, it was the largest and most important part of my world."[10]

Students participate in a lesson at a cramped segregated school, much like the one attended by Coretta and other African American students in the rural South before the rise of the civil rights movement.

Experiencing Racism

In addition to church, school was also an important part of Coretta's early life. She loved learning and proved to be an intelligent and hard-working student, excelling in all of her classes, especially music.

School, however, also provided Coretta with some of her earliest memories of discrimination. *New York Times* journalist Peter Applebome explains: "Some of Coretta Scott's earliest insights into the injustice of segregation came as she walked to her one-room school house each day, watching buses full of white children stir up dust as they passed."[11] Coretta's elementary school, Crossroads School, was a prime example of the discrimination that characterized the South. While white children attended school in a multiclassroom building, Coretta and other black children attended school in a one-room schoolhouse. The schoolhouse was an unpainted frame building with one big room, where over one hundred black children, from first grade through sixth, had their lessons. There was no electricity, no plumbing or indoor bathrooms, and little heat. A wood-burning stove provided the only warmth. The walls of the schoolhouse were painted black and used as a blackboard. Most of the black teachers had little college training but did the best they could to provide an education to the children.

In addition to the inferior conditions at school, Coretta also experienced discrimination personally on many other occasions. The drugstore, for example, where the children got ice cream bore signs saying "Whites Only." If black children wanted ice cream cones, they had to wait by the side door until all the white children had been served. Only then were the black children allowed ice cream, usually whatever flavor the store employee wanted to give them, rather than the flavor they desired. They paid the same price, however, as the white children. Later, when Coretta attended high school, she experienced additional problems. When she, her sister, and friends walked to school, they were often forced to walk in the street because white teenagers literally knocked them off the sidewalk.

Despite these experiences, Coretta admitted that her parents

The Jim Crow Era

Coretta Scott King grew up during a period of time known as the Jim Crow era. This era began in the late nineteenth century and ended in the mid-1950s. It was a time during which African Americans struggled to survive against racism, discrimination, and violence. The hardships endured by blacks resulted in widespread poverty, lack of education, and menial employment, especially in the southern states. Underlying this system was the belief that African Americans were inferior in every way to the white race.

After the Civil War ended, Southern blacks briefly enjoyed a period during which their civil rights were protected by federal laws and federal troops. As Southern states regained control of their governments, a number of laws were passed that severely curtailed or ended black rights, such as the right to vote and the right to hold public office. These laws, called Jim Crow laws, were accompanied by harassment, violence, and even murder in the form of lynching or hanging.

protected her, for the most part, from the worst of racism. From an early age, like other African American children, Coretta was taught that there were places where she just could not go and things she could not do. She knew, for instance, that she had to use the public restrooms that were marked for "Coloreds" and she knew to avoid any kind of interactions with whites.

Hardships and Threats

In addition to attending school and church, Coretta also started working outside her home at an early age. When she was ten years old, she went to work for a white cotton farmer to earn extra money for the family. She helped hoe long rows of cotton and picked cotton. The hours were long (sometimes twelve to fourteen hours a day) and hard; picking cotton was a backbreaking job. She earned between four and seven dollars for the entire cotton picking season, a fairly large amount of money at that time, especially for an African American. Coretta's longtime friend Andrew Young elaborates: "In thinking back on my memories of Coretta, I'm reminded that her father said she could pick two hundred pounds of cotton on a Saturday because she wanted to be able to stay up late to practice her music."[12]

Also at an early age, Coretta experienced the violence that typically accompanied racism in the South. The South, during Coretta's youth and for many years afterward, was a place characterized by racially motivated violence. The Scotts knew that at any moment they could be the target of such explosive feelings.

Self-sufficient blacks like Coretta's father were particularly at risk because they were usually perceived as a threat to white workers. Coretta's father, however, was a very proud man who refused to let the racism that he experienced break his spirit and his determination to succeed. Despite threats, her father was

Members of the Ku Klux Klan terrorized many African American families throughout the South in the early and mid 20th century with acts of intimidation and violence. The Scotts' family home and business were both destroyed in 1942 by fires set by the Klan.

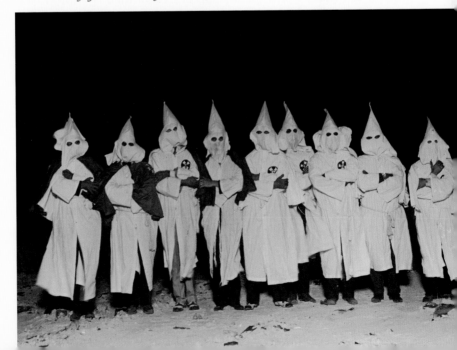

determined to succeed in the businesses he operated; he was equally determined to provide a decent life for his family. For his efforts, however, Obadiah Scott was thought to be "too uppity" by whites. Coretta explains: "During those . . . years, any African American who stood up like a man was considered uppity."[13]

One night a group of whites decided to punish Scott for being uppity. On Thanksgiving in 1942, the Scotts' house was set on fire and it burned to the ground. The family moved in with Coretta's maternal grandparents, the McMurrys, until the house could be rebuilt. In the meantime, Coretta's father, undaunted by the fire, purchased an old sawmill. Not long afterward, a white man demanded that Scott sell it to him. When Scott refused to do so,

Missionary Schools

King attended Lincoln High School in Marion, Alabama. Lincoln, like thousands of other black schools in the South, had been opened in the aftermath of the Civil War during the days of Reconstruction. Nearly four thousand such schools were built in the latter half of the nineteenth century. Many endured into the middle years of the twentieth century.

The majority of these schools were founded by various Northern church groups, including the American Missionary Society. The schools in the South were open to any African American who wanted an education. Students ranged in age from five to seventy. The majority of the teaching was done by white Northern teachers who had volunteered for the assignment.

For the first time in their history, Southern blacks had access to education. Prior to the Civil War, few African Americans in the South or elsewhere attended school. Slaves were forbidden to learn reading and writing. In addition, there were few schools anywhere that admitted black students. The creation of these missionary schools provided an opportunity for blacks to gain an education, something nearly all African Americans believed was necessary if they were to lead successful lives.

the sawmill burned down a few days later. Both fires were clearly arson, but neither crime was ever investigated nor was anyone ever punished, despite the fact that it was common knowledge that the local Ku Klux Klan, a white terrorist group intent on keeping blacks in their place, was responsible. Coretta later wrote: "My father's . . . unforgivable crime was that he worked too hard and got ahead—ahead of some of the poor whites."[14]

In addition to the loss of his house and sawmill, Obadiah Scott also faced danger personally. On numerous occasions he was stopped, while out in his truck, by whites who harassed and threatened him. Many of the poorer whites believed that they were out of work because of Scott's various jobs, especially hauling logs and lumber. Coretta later reported that she and her entire family never knew from one day to the next if their father would come home safely from a day's work. "I learned very early," she wrote, "to live with fear for the people I loved."[15]

Lincoln High School

Despite the hardships, the Scotts were determined that their children receive a good education. And despite their own lack of education, the Scotts, from early on, always instilled in their children a strong desire to learn. They were determined to send their children to college, no matter what sacrifices they might have to make. They believed that an education would provide their children with a better chance of success and advancement in the white man's world. Bernice Scott told her daughter: "You are just as good as anyone else . . . you get an education and try to be somebody. Then you won't have to be kicked around by anybody and you won't have to depend on anyone for your livelihood, not even on a man."[16]

To ensure that their children were properly educated, the Scotts sent them to nearby Lincoln High School in Marion, Alabama. Lincoln was a private, African American high school that had been named after President Abraham Lincoln by a group of ex-slaves, who had then appealed to the American Missionary Association in the late 1860s for help in providing both money and teachers for the school. Since that time, the school had become well-known as a place where African American children could attend school past the sixth grade. It had an excellent reputation because so many of its graduates continued their education in universities across the country.

Coretta and her siblings were in the minority; few blacks in the South were able to attend high school at all. Since blacks were refused admission to white high schools, and few black high schools existed, many blacks had no place to go to further their education. In addition, farming needs often took precedence over education for the majority of African American families living in the South.

Because Lincoln High was 12 miles (19km) away from the Scotts' home, Coretta and her sister Edythe stayed with a black family in Marion. By the time Coretta was a junior, her father had converted a truck into a bus, thus providing transportation that enabled Coretta and her sister to live at home and ride to school.

Coretta was in the seventh grade when she started at Lincoln. For the first time, she saw black and white teachers working together. One of the teachers she met there was Olive Williams. Williams saw the musical talent in the young girl and helped Coretta develop into a fine singer and musician. As a result, Coretta learned to play the piano, violin, and other instruments. In addition, she participated in various musical programs at the school. Williams also gave Coretta her first voice lessons and encouraged the teenager to perform vocal solos with the school chorus. As her singing and other musical talents improved, Coretta began to dream about pursuing some kind of career in music.

Coretta, throughout her life, praised Lincoln High School for helping her find the confidence to pursue a higher education. Coretta later told reporters: "The chance to go to such a school made a real difference in my life . . . Lincoln opened the world to me."[17]

Chapter 2

Preparing for a Musical Career

Coretta Scott King graduated from Lincoln High School in the spring of 1945. She had already decided to follow her sister, Edythe, and attend Antioch College, a small liberal arts college in Ohio. Edthye, two years older than Coretta, had earned a scholarship to Antioch and wrote glowing letters to her sister about the open atmosphere and the lack of discrimination she found in the North.

King, like her sister, knew that if she wanted a quality college education, she would have to leave the South. Most Southern universities at that time were all white. While there were a number of good black universities, King decided she wanted to take advantage of the opportunities afforded in the North. Like her sister, King also received a scholarship to attend Antioch, where she hoped to enjoy a far greater amount of freedom than she had experienced in Alabama.

Life at Antioch

In the fall of 1945, King arrived at Antioch, located in the small Ohio town of Yellow Springs. She received a friendly welcome from the predominantly white student body there. The student body was, in fact, overwhelmingly white; King and her sister were among only six blacks enrolled at the university.

King decided to study elementary education and music,

University archivists look over photos and books of Coretta inside the Antioch College library. Although Coretta was one of only six African Americans enrolled at the campus, she enjoyed the campus's open atmosphere and took advantage of many educational opportunities offered there.

and thus declared a double major in those two areas. She was impressed with Antioch's open atmosphere and flexible study program. She was able to work with various teachers to design her own course of study, and she decided to participate in the college's work-study program. This involved studying for half the

Antioch College

Antioch College was founded in 1852. The small liberal arts college is located in Yellow Springs, Ohio. Horace Mann, a man widely known for his fight against slavery, was the first president of the college. He believed that educating men and women of both races would only serve to make the United States stronger. Throughout its history Antioch has been known for its support of and connection to antislavery campaigns, equal rights groups, and social justice activists.

Antioch would later become one of the first colleges to enroll an interracial student body. Journalist James Hannah explains: "Antioch was fertile ground for thinking and discussion of civil rights and other social issues. Activism and civil disobedience became part of the fabric of the school, with anti-war protests in the 1960s and 70s to the student takeover of the administration building in the 1990s." The college has remained committed to offering innovative study programs and to being politically and socially active.

Antioch today has a cultural center named for its 1951 graduate, Coretta Scott King. In February 2008, university officials announced that the school would temporarily close its doors in June 2008, but will reopen in the near future. The reasons for this are financial and low enrollment.

James Hannah, "Coretta Scott King Left Mark at Ohio College," *Cincinnati Post*, February 8, 2006.

A student walks past the administration building at Antioch College in Yellow Springs, Ohio, the school from which Coretta graduated in 1951.

year and working the other half. It took longer to earn a degree but the plan enabled her to earn money that helped offset some of her living expenses.

In addition to working in the music library and the college dining hall, King also held jobs as a nursery school teacher, social worker, and camp counselor. She also worked during the summer months to increase her experience.

During the summer of her freshman year, King worked as a junior music counselor at Karamu Camp. The camp was operated by the Karamu House of Cleveland, Ohio, a nonprofit organization that stressed arts and education and encouraged the celebration of African American culture. The following summer, she worked at the Friendly Inn Settlement House, located in one of Cleveland's poorest neighborhoods. This facility catered to poor black women and their children. These two experiences opened King's eyes to the poverty and difficult lives that northern blacks, just like their counterparts in the South, endured.

Discrimination

Despite the overall friendliness of the students and the warm welcome she received at Antioch and in other northern cities, King, nonetheless, experienced many forms of discrimination while in college. She reported that she was aware, almost from the beginning, that many of the white students felt somewhat superior to her, based solely on the fact that they were white and she was not. "People were nice to me," King later wrote, "and tried to be friendly but I could sense that in the backs of their minds was the feeling of race superiority bred in them through generations and by all the myths about black people they had acquired."[18]

Discrimination also reared its ugly head when it came time for King to do her practice teaching. The public schools in Yellow Springs were integrated and contained both white and black students, but there were no black teachers. She was told that she would have to work in the all-black schools of nearby Xenia, Ohio. This did not sit well with King, who was quite disillusioned and upset. She told school officials she would not go to Xenia and reminded them that she had come north to escape segregation, not continue to participate in it.

King even went to see the college president. She asked him to take steps to rectify the situation but he refused. "Her protests fell on deaf ears," AfricanAmericans.com explains, "even when she appealed to the college president, and in the end she had to do her teaching at the Antioch Demonstration School, an elementary school established by the college for students in the Yellow Springs area."[19] Despite her disappointment, King enjoyed her practice teaching. She took a personal interest in her young students, composing and singing songs to them.

This experience heightened King's awareness of the racism that existed even in the North. Following this incident, King pledged to fight for social justice issues and joined the campus NAACP (National Association for the Advancement of Colored People). While at Antioch, she also became a member of the university's race relations and civil liberties committee, a group that monitored and tried to improve race relations and other civil rights issues on campus. King promised herself that she would continue the fight against discrimination after graduation. She elaborates: "From the first I had been determined to get ahead, not just for myself, but to do something for my people and for all people."[20] From that point onward, she dedicated herself to finding a career that combined musical performances with social activism.

A Promising Musician

In the meantime, King continued her studies. Through the music courses she took, King came to the attention of Dr. Walter Anderson, the head of the music department and the only African American professor at Antioch. Anderson immediately took notice of King's exceptional musical abilities and encouraged her to broaden her musical education. He became King's mentor and spent extra time with her overseeing her voice lessons and encouraging her to expand her musical abilities. Anderson also encouraged her to sing in college musicals as well as with the university chorus.

Through her hard work and study, King was becoming a very proficient singer and musician. With Anderson's encouragement, she made her professional singing debut in 1948 at a concert in Springfield, Ohio, at the Second Baptist Church. She was part of a program that included other professional singers. Her performance came to the attention of noted performer and social activist, Paul Robeson, who was also on the program. Robeson was a renowned singer and actor, as well as an outspoken critic of segregation. He was so moved by her singing and her wonderful soprano voice that he encouraged the young singer to pursue a career in music. As a result of the conversation she had with Robeson and because of the audience's response, King decided to become a professional concert singer and musician.

As her graduation from Antioch approached, King began to investigate ways of continuing her musical education. With the help of Anderson and others, she focused her attention on two schools—the Juilliard School in New York City and the New

African American singer, actor, and social activist Paul Robeson was impressed with Coretta's singing talent after seeing her perform in 1948, and he urged her to pursue a musical career.

Famed African American contralto Marian Anderson performs at the Lincoln Memorial in Washington, D.C., on Easter Sunday 1939, a nationally broadcast event that was arranged by her supporters after she was denied permission to sing at Constitution Hall. Coretta's studies at the New England Conservatory of Music were inspired by her admiration of Anderson.

England Conservatory of Music in Boston, two of the top music schools in the United States. She ultimately decided to attend the conservatory when she was offered a scholarship. While she had enjoyed teaching, she firmly believed her true calling was in the field of music.

Trip to Boston

After graduating from Antioch in 1951, King returned briefly to Alabama and worked for her father for the summer. She told her family and friends that attending Antioch had been a good decision. Journalist Vicki Crawford, writing for the *Journal of African American History*, elaborates on the importance of Antioch: "Coretta Scott blossomed [at Antioch] intellectually and politically, deepening the values and orientation that shaped the full course of her young life. Antioch strengthened the self-confidence of the intelligent, yet unexposed young woman."[21]

In the fall of 1951, King left for Boston where she would be one of twenty black students at the New England Conservatory of Music. While her scholarship covered tuition, it did not, however, pay for room and board. Friends from Antioch had arranged for her to live with a wealthy white woman, Mrs. Bartol, while in Boston. This helped offset some of her expenses, but King still struggled to make ends meet. She and Mrs. Bartol eventually came to an agreement—King would do the cleaning in exchange for meals. As AfricanAmericans.com explains: "To pay for her bed and breakfast, she cleaned the stairwells of the house she lived in, and for supper she usually made do with peanut butter and crackers."[22]

The Urban League, a civil rights organization dedicated to helping African Americans, also helped her find a part-time job with a mail-order company. Finally, during her second year in Boston, the state of Alabama began sending money. Since southern states would not allow black students to attend all-white universities, they were ultimately forced by the federal government to give financial aid to African American students who were attending colleges elsewhere.

At the conservatory, King studied voice and music with a former Metropolitan opera singer as well as other noted performers. In addition, she sang with the choir at the Old South Church and took part in musical programs presented by the conservatory. Longtime friend Andrew Young elaborates: "Coretta Scott was already a woman of purpose when she enrolled in the New England Conservatory of Music in Boston. Her purpose: to follow in the footsteps of Marian Anderson as a concert singer."[23] Marian Anderson was a noted black singer who had been forbidden to sing to an integrated audience in a Washington, D.C. concert hall in 1939. With the help of First Lady Eleanor Roosevelt, Anderson later appeared at the Lincoln Memorial and captivated the audience as well as the nation. King hoped to pursue just such a career.

A Special Date

While pursuing her career, King's good friend and fellow music student, Mary Powell, suggested that King date a friend of hers from Atlanta. Powell described a young man who was intent on a career in the ministry and who, at that time, was pursuing a doctorate degree at Boston University. At first, King was not inclined to even talk to the young man. She had become disillusioned with organized religion and was not particularly interested in meeting

Martin Luther King Jr.'s Early Life

Martin Luther King Jr. was born on January 15, 1929, in Atlanta, Georgia. He was the son of well-known minister Martin Luther King Sr., who was a strong advocate for the black community. As a child, Martin often imitated his father by preaching to his teddy bears. Unlike Coretta who grew up poor in rural Alabama, Martin grew up in a middle-class home in the center of Atlanta. Their different upbringings exposed them to different forms of discrimination and racism.

Martin graduated from Morehouse College in Atlanta and then attended Crozer, a college for ministers in Pennsylvania. He found the purpose of his ministry after attending a lecture about the life of Mahatma Gandhi who had led the people of India in nonviolent protests against the British government. He was determined to lead his own people to the same kind of freedom—in this case, equality and an end to segregation. He was in Boston studying for a doctor of philosophy degree when he met Coretta Scott.

Martin's father was originally not in favor of his marrying Coretta. He wanted his son to marry into a family with money and had several prominent Atlanta beauties in mind. Martin, however, was determined to choose his own wife and made it clear that Coretta Scott was his choice.

him. She ultimately told Powell, however, that she would at least talk to him and then make a decision.

On Powell's advice, the young man, Martin Luther King Jr., called King and said: "A mutual friend of ours told me about you and gave me your telephone number. She said some wonderful things about you and I'd like very much to meet you and talk to you."[24] After talking for a few minutes, King agreed to meet him the next day for lunch.

When he pulled up to her residence and got out of the car, the first thing King noticed was his size. She later wrote: "My first thought was how short he seemed, and the second was how unimpressive he was."[25] Her first impression was soon forgotten. As they talked during that first date, she quickly became aware of his intelligence and his charm. By the end of the date, she knew he was a special person. King later said that after a few minutes in his presence, "I had forgotten about Martin being short and had completely revised my first impression. He radiated charm. When he talked, he grew in stature. Even when he was so young, he drew people to him from the very first moment with his eloquence, his sincerity, and his moral stature."[26]

Martin Luther King Jr., for his part, was completely captivated by King's charm and intelligence. Martin, in fact, surprised her at the end of that first date by announcing: "The four things that I look for in a wife are character, personality, intelligence, and beauty. And you have them all."[27] King Jr. himself would later write: "It was in Boston that I met and fell in love with the attractive singer, Coretta Scott, whose gentle manner and air of repose did not disguise her lively spirit."[28]

Coretta and Martin dated frequently during the next few months, attending concerts, going to movies, and dancing. Above all, they talked and got to know one another. They also discovered that they both shared the same dream of wanting to use their education to help others, especially the poor.

A Momentous Decision

When Martin proposed a few months later, Coretta waited six months before saying yes. While feeling very attracted to him, she was torn between that attraction and her desire to pursue a career in music. Her first priorities had always been her singing and music but after meeting Martin, she was forced to reconsider her goals.

To help her decide, King traveled south to Atlanta to meet Martin's parents. She met them and also attended Ebenezer Baptist Church where Martin's father was the pastor. Martin's father, called "Daddy King" by the family, was an imposing man. Originally, he wanted his son to marry an Atlanta girl, but after meeting Coretta, he changed his mind. The elder King was impressed with Coretta's intelligence and her beliefs about civil rights. He came to believe that Coretta would be the perfect wife for his son. He

Ebenezer Baptist Church in Atlanta, Georgia, was headed in the 1950s by Reverend Martin Luther King Sr., who wanted his son Martin to marry a local girl. Upon meeting Coretta, who attended services at the church during her visit to meet Martin's parents, King Sr. gave his blessing to the couple.

would later admit that Coretta's support had enabled his son to become the great leader that he was.

Following the trip south, King prayed and thought about her decision and ultimately decided that, yes, she did want marriage and a family. In addition to the deep love she felt for him, King was also attracted by the fact that she and Martin shared a special vision of being able to help their fellow African Americans; they were both dedicated to changing the status quo. She found Martin highly intelligent and committed to civil rights and was very impressed with his sense of mission. King came to believe that she had been led to Boston for the purpose of meeting Martin Luther King Jr. and that their lives were meant to be lived together.

One big concern, however, remained. Before saying yes, she talked with Martin about the role she would play in their marriage. A very independent woman, King wanted to be an equal partner in the relationship, not just a behind-the-scenes wife. She saw herself and Martin as a team; a team committed to making the world a better place.

Martin, however, wanted a more traditional wife. He told her that he did not want a career wife and was opposed to her working outside the home other than in the role of a minister's wife. She ultimately decided to accept his role of family leader and told him she would, in fact, marry him. Despite his assertions of wanting a stay-at-home wife, he readily agreed later that she was much more; that, in fact, she was a full partner and participant in his work, not just a supporting wife.

Wedding and Early Marriage

Martin and Coretta were married on June 18, 1953, in the garden of her parents' home in Alabama. She wore a long blue dress trimmed with lace. They exchanged their vows in front of family and friends in a ceremony presided over by Martin's father. According to *New York Times* journalist, Peter Applebome, "she stunned Dr. King's father, the Reverend Martin Luther King, Sr., who presided over the wedding, by demanding that the 'promise to obey' her husband be removed from the wedding vows."[29] Martin fully supported her decision.

Following a reception, the newly married couple spent an unusual wedding night. Newspaper reporter Zenitha Prince elaborates: "[They] spent their wedding night in a funeral home because White-owned hotels would not accommodate them."[30] The couple would joke about this for years. The next day, they traveled from Alabama to Atlanta, Georgia, and moved in with the elder Kings for the remainder of the summer.

Upon returning from the South in the fall, they rented a four-room house in Boston. Coretta was taking thirteen courses in order to finish her degree in music education with a major in voice. She was also learning to play a number of different instruments, as well as taking instruction in choir directing. She did some practice teaching in her last semester and, unlike her experience in Yellow Springs, found that the white students in Boston accepted a black teacher without difficulty.

In the meantime, Martin was finishing his doctorate. He needed only to work on his thesis, a long written composition required of PhD candidates. While Coretta attended school, Martin stayed in their home and worked on his writing. He also did most of the cleaning and cooking during this time, freeing up his young wife to complete her education. He also preached at a number of Boston churches, gaining confidence in his ministerial abilities.

Chapter 3

Montgomery

By early 1954, Coretta had her advanced degree in music and Martin was close to completing his dissertation. The young couple began to talk about their future plans. Martin had offers of employment from colleges, businesses, and large churches in both the North and the South. While the North afforded greater financial opportunities and less racism, both Kings were inclined to return to the South.

The *Brown v. Board of Education* ruling by the Supreme Court that proclaimed segregated schools unconstitutional had just been handed down, and the Kings wanted to take part in the desegregation of public schools in the South. In addition, both their roots and their families were down South. The biggest factor, however, was that both Martin and Coretta wanted to serve their people in some capacity. Martin elaborates: "Finally, we agreed that, in spite of the disadvantages and inevitable sacrifices, our greatest service could be rendered in our native South."[31] Coretta played a significant role in their decision. Andrew Young explains: "The fact that [Martin] came back South with his Boston Ph.D., rather than pursue another course, was as much a product of Coretta's commitment and dedication to change the South as Martin's."[32]

A Minister's Wife

After much prayer and discussion, the Kings selected a job opportunity at Dexter Avenue Baptist Church in Montgomery, Alabama,

Martin wears his vestments outside of the Dexter Avenue Baptist Church in Montgomery, Alabama, where he was named pastor in 1954 at the age of twenty-five.

where Martin had been offered the job of pastor. Dexter Avenue Baptist Church sat in the city square and had been built during the days of Reconstruction following the Civil War. It seated four hundred people; primarily affluent college-educated blacks, many of whom were professionals.

The Kings moved into a small-frame house with seven rooms that the church provided in a nearby segregated neighborhood. One of their first purchases was a piano so that Coretta could continue her music and singing. From the beginning of their lives in Montgomery, she sang with the church choir. She also served as Martin's secretary and served on a number of church committees.

In addition to writing his sermons, Martin also continued work on his thesis and finally obtained his PhD in June 1955. Martin also quickly gained recognition among the congregation as a friendly and inspiring minister. Many of his sermons were about fear. "In the South," Coretta explains, "[fear] was our greatest problem. Racists, and groups like the Ku Klux Klan and even the police used fear as their weapon to keep blacks down."[33]

On November 19, 1955, Coretta gave birth to their first child; a daughter who was named Yolanda Denise, but called "Yoki." Yoki was born at St. Jude's Hospital, a Catholic institution and the only hospital in Montgomery where blacks could get decent treatment. Many other hospitals refused to even admit African Americans.

The Bus Boycott

Coretta and Martin's life changed dramatically in late 1955. Martin had, since their arrival in Montgomery, been working with other African American ministers and leaders in trying to end many of the unfair segregation laws of that city. One of the biggest problems they faced was segregation on city buses. Black riders were required by law to sit in the back of the bus. In addition, they were also required to give up their seats if whites needed seating. Coretta elaborates: "Of all the facets of segregation in Montgomery, the most degrading were the rules of the

Two white women are the only passengers on a bus in Montgomery, Alabama, after African Americans stopped using the transit system in December 1955 to protest the degrading rules that dictated where on the bus they could sit.

Montgomery City Bus Lines. . . . Although 70% of its passengers were black, it treated them like cattle."[34]

This issue was brought to a climax on December 1 when tailor's assistant, Rosa Parks, after a particularly long day, refused to give up her seat on a city bus when asked to do so by the bus driver. The driver, James P. Blake, called the police. A group of policemen then met the bus at the next stop and arrested Parks for disobeying the city's law. News of her arrest spread quickly throughout the black community.

That same evening, Martin met with other black church leaders to discuss Parks's arrest. Unanimously, they decided that the best course of action was to boycott the city buses. They asked the black community, by word of mouth, to refrain from riding the buses and to find other ways to work. The group of ministers named themselves the Montgomery Improvement Association and elected King, age twenty-six, as the president. They set Monday, December 5 as the day the boycott would begin.

Rosa Parks

Many historians date the beginning of the civil rights movement to December 1, 1955, the day that seamstress Rosa Parks refused to give up her seat on a Montgomery, Alabama, bus. Journalist Heather Gray elaborates: "Mrs. Parks was known as the mother of the civil rights movement. By refusing to walk to the back of the bus in Montgomery in 1955, she launched the modern civil rights era."

Rosa McCauley Parks was born in Tuskegee, Alabama, in 1913. She later attended Alabama State Teacher's College and ultimately settled in Montgomery with her husband Raymond Parks. As a secretary to the president of the local National Association for the Advancement of Colored People (NAACP), Parks worked quietly to improve conditions for African Americans. The bus incident brought her worldwide media coverage. More importantly, her act of defiance led to the successful bus boycott that triggered the civil rights movement.

Later, she and her husband moved to Detroit, Michigan, where she served on the staff of U.S. Representative John Conyers. She is also credited with founding the Rosa and Raymond Parks Institute for Self-Development, an organization that provides programs for African American teenagers. On October 24, 2005, she died at the age of ninety-two and was honored by the government; her casket lay in state in the Rotunda of the U.S. Capitol for two days. She was the first woman in American history to receive this honor.

Rosa Parks is fingerprinted in the months following her December 1955 arrest for refusing to give up her seat on a Montgomery, Alabama, city bus to a white passenger, an act of defiance that is said to mark the beginning of the civil rights movement in the U.S.

Heather Gray, "Remembering Coretta Scott King, the Untiring Advocate for Justice," *Atlanta Inquirer*, February 2, 2006.

Word of the boycott spread from the pulpit of black churches in Montgomery and also through newspapers, both black and white. Martin and Coretta waited anxiously to see how the African American community would respond. The Kings were up early that Monday morning waiting for the first city bus to pass their home. Martin later wrote about that morning and stated that he was in the kitchen when he heard his wife call out: "Martin, Martin, come quickly. . . . Darling, it's empty."[35] No blacks were on the bus; nor were there any on the next several buses that came by their home. Coretta later told reporters: "Right on time, the bus came, headlights blazing through the December darkness, all lit up inside. . . . There was not one person on that usually crowded bus."[36]

The Bombing

During the first few weeks of the boycott, and continuing over the next several months, hundreds of threatening phone calls came into the King house, in addition to thousands of pieces of hate mail. Other civil rights leaders in Montgomery received similar threats. Coretta, having grown up facing the threats against her father, knew that their situation was extremely dangerous. The white people of Montgomery were furious; no blacks had ever tried anything so bold in the past. "We never felt we were safe at any point,"[37] Coretta told reporters.

Martin was gone a good deal of the time, speaking at various functions and meeting with other members of the Montgomery Improvement Association. He was particularly concerned about leaving Coretta at home alone with a newborn baby. Coretta arranged for friends to stay with her on occasion, most of whom were members of the Dexter Avenue Baptist Church congregation.

On the evening of January 30, 1956, while Martin was speaking at a nearby church, the Kings' fears were realized. Coretta and a friend were sitting in the living room when they heard a loud noise on the porch, as if something had been thrown there. Immediately recognizing the potential for trouble, Coretta and

Martin stands with local police officials on the front porch of his home in January 1956, urging the largely African American crowd that had assembled before him to remain calm in response to the news that the King home had been firebombed.

her friend moved toward the back of the house where baby Yoki was sleeping. They had just reached a back bedroom when the house was rocked by a huge explosion, followed by the sound of breaking glass and the smell of smoke. A bomb had exploded on the Kings' front porch, leaving a huge hole there, as well as doing massive damage to the window and front room.

Fortunately, Coretta, her friend, and the baby were all safe. Neighbors immediately flocked to the home to see if Coretta was all right, while Martin heard the news from a colleague while still at the nearby church. He was immediately assured that his family had not been injured. Upon arriving home, he immediately sought them out. "When I walked into the bedroom and saw my wife and daughter uninjured, I drew my first full breath in many minutes. Coretta was neither bitter nor panicky."[38] Her bravery, and her awareness that such an incident might occur, had enabled her to meet the threat and survive.

He also found a huge crowd outside his house. White police-men were present, but the majority of the people there were black. Martin feared that the smallest incident would set off vio-lence. He and Coretta were both aware that if violence did break out, a riot could easily follow with a loss of life. Because of this, he spoke to the crowd and asked them to stay peaceful. Martin's words quieted the crowd, and it soon dispersed.

Coretta's father arrived the next day and told her that he was taking her and Yoki home with him. Coretta refused to go, tell-ing him that her place was with her husband. Martin and others later spoke of Coretta's courage in making this decision. As for Coretta, she reports that after the bombing: "I knew at that point that being with him, and participating in this Movement, was the right thing for me. I was able to draw strength from my religious beliefs."[39]

Within days, floodlights had been erected around their house. In addition, the congregation at Dexter hired a night watchman to guard the home, especially when Martin was away. From that time onward, someone always stayed with Coretta when Martin was away.

A Courageous Woman

The bus boycott continued for over a year; it lasted 381 days. People from all over the United States, both black and white, sent money to the Montgomery Improvement Association. Almost overnight, Martin became the leader of African American activism and a well-known figure throughout the United States. Newsmen and other visitors began to come to their home to visit and listen to Martin; they were always welcomed into the home. Coretta welcomed and treated everyone like family, going out of her way to feed anyone who showed up.

The longer the boycott went on, the angrier the white gov-ernment of Montgomery became. An attempt to break the boy-cott by arresting the black leaders backfired. The arrests merely strengthened everyone's determination to succeed. Coretta, in an interview on public radio, never questioned their involvement.

She stated: "I never thought of it as a sacrifice during the time I was involved. I thought of it as a commitment. I had a very strong and deep commitment to the struggle. Starting in my college days, I was an activist. . . . I went to my first political convention in 1948 as a student delegate, and so when Montgomery started it was just natural for me to feel very much involved."[40]

During the boycott, danger was ever present and the Kings frequently talked of the possibility that Martin might be injured or killed. Despite these fears, however, Coretta continued to fully support him and the civil rights movement. As Martin's exposure increased, so too did the threats made against him. Coretta, however, remained courageous throughout the turmoil, as Martin explains: "In the midst of the most tragic experiences, she never

Coretta greets Martin with a kiss outside of a Montgomery, Alabama, courthouse in March 1956 after his trial on conspiracy charges that were brought about by local officials trying to force an end to the bus boycott. He was found guilty, but the judge suspended his fine.

became panicky or over-emotional. . . . While she had certain natural fears and anxieties concerning my welfare, she never allowed them to hamper my active participation in the movement."[41]

Andrew Young, who later became a U.S. congressman, the mayor of Atlanta, and the first African American ambassador to the United Nations, was with the Kings for much of the civil rights movement. He praised Coretta's courage and commitment to the cause of civil rights: "I never heard her complain about anything. It was as though she was born for the breadth and depth of responsibility that she incurred as the wife of Martin Luther King, Jr.; she was as strong, if not stronger than he was."[42]

Meanwhile, the boycott continued. The absence of black riders on the bus lines resulted in financial hardship for the City of Montgomery and city leaders looked for some way to end the boycott without actually giving in to the demands of the black leaders. Late in December 1956, the decision was taken out of their hands when the U.S. Supreme Court ruled that Montgomery's bus laws were unconstitutional and ordered the city to end segregation. On December 20, 1956, the mayor of Montgomery announced he would comply with the ruling. The success in Montgomery led to boycotts and protests in other Southern cities. Step by step, city by city, segregation was slowly beginning to end throughout the South.

Once the boycott had ended, Coretta, in an effort to celebrate and tell the story of the boycott, appeared in New York City at the Manhattan Center with black entertainers such as Harry Belafonte and Duke Ellington. Coretta, however, was the featured performer. After singing several classical pieces, she then told the story of the Montgomery bus boycott in both words and songs. Her performance won her a standing ovation.

Trip to Ghana

With the bus boycott settled to their satisfaction, Martin and Coretta left Montgomery a few months later and traveled to the African country of Ghana. They went with thousands of other dignitaries who were celebrating the country's independence from Great Britain.

Dr. Kwame Nkrumah, the Ghanian leader, welcomed the Kings to his country like they were royalty. While there, the Kings attended the celebration along with fifty thousand Ghanians, many of whom wore the colorful robes of their native tribes, as Nkrumah spoke of the long fight for independence. Martin and Coretta were both inspired by the words they heard.

At midnight on March 5, 1957, the bells of the capital city of Accra began to ring. Then the red, white, and blue flag of Great Britain and a symbol of colonial dependency came down. In its place, the new Ghana flag of green, gold, and red was raised to the accompanying cheers of the crowd.

The Kings wept along with Nkrumah, knowing that black people in both the United States and Africa were beginning to move forward toward independence and freedom. Nkrumah would later tell the Kings how the bus boycott in Montgomery had

Coretta, left, and Martin, center, are gifted with garlands by admirers after landing in New Delhi, India, for a tour of the nation in February 1959.

Southern Christian Leadership Conference

The Montgomery bus boycott was led by two dynamic ministers: Martin Luther King Jr. and Ralph David Abernathy. The men—and their wives—became good friends.

In January 1957 King and Abernathy joined sixty other black church activists in Atlanta to create the Southern Christian Leadership Conference (SCLC), a group that dedicated themselves to the use of nonviolence in achieving equality. The group was composed primarily of leaders from African American churches in the South. King was nominated and served as the group's first president.

The organization's primary focus in the early years of the civil rights movement was on voter registration and the desegregation of the South's public schools. The group also played an active role in many other events during the 1950s and 1960s, including the March on Washington in 1963.

Following her husband's death, Coretta Scott King served on the board of directors for a brief time but later came in conflict with the group over her decision to proceed with the King Center. The SCLC complained that the money she raised could have been better used elsewhere.

given him the inspiration to move forward. The Kings returned home, committed to continuing their own fight toward equality and integration. Coretta summarized their feelings: "It was an intensely thrilling moment for Martin and me. We felt a strong sense of identity and kinship with those African people shouting 'Freedom.'"[43]

The Harlem Incident

Not long after their return to Montgomery, Coretta helped her husband write the book, *Stride Toward Freedom*, about the events that had taken place during the boycott. Martin dedicated the book to his wife. Following the book's publication in 1958, Martin embarked on a tour to promote interest in the book.

Coretta stayed at home with their two young children (Martin Luther King III had been born on October 23, 1957). She was preparing a meal when she got a frantic telephone call from one of her husband's associates. She learned that Martin had been stabbed during a book signing in Harlem, New York. Leaving her children with friends, she immediately rushed to his side at Harlem Hospital.

There, she learned how serious the injury was. He had been stabbed with a very sharp letter opener by a distraught black woman, who was later found to be mentally ill. Coretta was told that her husband had been forced to lay waiting for the ambulance with the opener still in his chest. The doctors informed her that part of the weapon was touching his aorta, the large artery leading to the heart. The surgeon, Aubre D. Maynard, stated that if Martin had moved or sneezed, he would have probably died instantly. Despite the attack on her husband, Coretta told reporters that while they lived under a constant threat, they both believed the work they were doing was important enough to die for.

After saying a silent prayer of thanks, Coretta got to work. She approached hospital executives and requested a number of offices on the first floor for her use. There, she set about answering the numerous phone calls and letters that poured into the hospital about her husband and his condition. While in New York, she also carried on the civil rights work he had been scheduled to do before being hospitalized. In addition to completing Martin's work in New York City, Coretta also participated in a protest march in Washington, D.C. and even gave a speech that her husband had written for the occasion.

After Martin had recuperated from his injuries, the couple decided to take some time off from their civil rights work. They traveled to India where they witnessed the extreme poverty of that nation. Both Martin and Coretta decided to address the issue of American poverty, especially among African Americans, when they returned to the United States.

While in India, they also met with government officials and visited the sites that Mahatma Gandhi had made famous. Gandhi's use of nonviolence in obtaining independence for India from Great Britain inspired Martin's own ideals. While visiting these places, Martin took the opportunity to speak out against discrimination in many places, while Coretta often appeared on the same stages and sang. Martin later joked with reporters, telling them that the crowds had applauded more for his wife's singing than for anything he said.

The Decision to Move On

As the 1950s came to a close, the Kings were busier than ever. Martin was spending more and more time away from home, especially in Atlanta, Georgia. Atlanta had become the headquarters of the Southern Christian Leadership Conference (SCLC), a group dedicated to nonviolent protest. As president of that organization, Martin was in Atlanta more than he was in Montgomery.

Martin and Coretta were also dealing with a trial. A Montgomery jury had indicted Martin on a charge of falsifying a state income tax return. The charges stated that Martin had received money from both the Montgomery Improvement Association and the SCLC that he had not claimed on his tax return. While the charges were completely false, the Kings held little hope of an acquittal, because of the all-white jury. They were, therefore, completely astonished when the jury returned a verdict of not guilty. While the trial had exonerated Martin, the Kings both felt emotionally exhausted after it was over.

The couple began to seriously consider a move. Martin felt that he was not doing justice to his job at Dexter Avenue Baptist Church because of his frequent absences and suggested that they move to Atlanta to be closer to the SCLC organization. After he was offered the opportunity to be copastor along with his father at Ebenezer Baptist Church in Atlanta, the Kings decided to leave Montgomery.

Chapter 4

Triumph and Tragedy

In Atlanta Coretta continued in her role as a minister's wife, a mother, and a coworker in the civil rights movement. Marian Wright Edelman, founder of the Children's Defense Fund, elaborates: "Her own activism and deep commitment to civil rights made her an ideal partner. . . . She often took on a behind-the-scenes role, staying at home with their four children while Dr. King traveled as a public leader. But in the most important battles of the civil rights movement, she was always right there by her husband's side."[44] In fact, Coretta took part in many of the marches with Martin; she is often pictured walking hand in hand with her husband. In August 1963 Coretta sat behind Martin as he gave the moving "I Have a Dream" speech in Washington, D.C. She and the crowd of over 250,000 people cheered as Martin delivered his stirring words. The speech helped propel the civil rights movement forward, as thousands of blacks and whites joined in the fight. Many sent money, and many took an active role in various civil rights activities, while others allowed their hearts to be changed.

Behind the Scenes

Far more often, however, Coretta was home with the children, working diligently to provide them with a stable home life in the midst of the turmoil that accompanied the civil rights movement. The Kings' third child, Dexter Scott, was born in early 1961, while their fourth child, Bernice Albertine (called Bunny) was born in 1963. With her husband traveling an estimated 300,000 miles (48,280km) a year and giving over four hundred speeches

Because Martin's work frequently took him away from home, Coretta was charged with maintaining the household and ensuring stability for their children. Here she packs a picnic basket with the three oldest King children in August 1962 during one of several jail stints Martin endured during the civil rights movement.

around the country, it was left to Coretta to maintain the home front and raise the children.

Coretta always tried to provide as normal a childhood as possible for her children. Dexter describes their home and his mother's role: "Our home at 234 Sunset was kind of home central. The neighborhood headquarters. All the kids came by to play. My mom treated them like hers . . . [she] was a disciplinarian, took no guff from hers or any other [kids]."[45]

In addition to the praise that she received from her children, others also applauded Coretta's efforts. Senator Edward M. Kennedy of Massachusetts once stated: "I've had the good opportunity to get to know the children over the years and I have seen the time that they spent with their mother. The mother was not only a powerful and charismatic figure . . . but she helped those children grow up to be individuals with a sense of dignity, a sense of pride in their heritage, and their strong commitment to do something for someone else."[46]

Family time was special because it came so infrequently. Martin admitted that family moments were rare. "We could never plan for them, for I seldom knew from one hour to the next when I would be home. Many times, Coretta saw her good meals grow dry in the oven, when a sudden emergency kept me away. Yet she never complained, and she was always there when I needed her. . . . When I needed to talk things out, she was ready to listen, or to offer suggestions when I asked for them."[47] Despite Martin's busy schedule, the family always had a special celebration during the holidays and on the children's birthdays.

Providing a normal childhood was made more difficult by the times in which the Kings lived. It was a daunting job for African American parents to bring up their children in the South during the 1950s and 1960s. Harassment, prejudice, discrimination, and violence were everyday occurrences. Despite these hardships, the Kings brought up their children to believe that they were just as good as any other children.

Freedom Concerts

In addition to rearing her children and supporting Martin in his endeavors, Coretta, beginning in the early 1960s, also took a far more active role in the civil rights movement. Her primary method of activism was by performing in a number of freedom concerts at various sites throughout the country. Her first one was given in 1964 at New York City's Town Hall. Similar to the program she had given after the bus boycott's success, the concerts featured songs, poetry, and narration, all of which Coretta wrote and performed. She talked about various civil rights events and

Coretta speaks of the struggle for civil rights before her performance at a Freedom Concert in Trenton, New Jersey, in October 1965. By the end of the 1960s, she had given more than 30 such performances and had raised over $50,000 for the Southern Christian Leadership Conference.

The March on Washington

On August 28, 1963, Martin Luther King Jr. led a march down the Washington, D.C. mall to the Lincoln Memorial. On the steps of the monument, Martin gave his famous "I Have a Dream" speech to a crowd of 250,000 people who had come from all over America to participate in the march.

The idea for this event came from Coretta who, in early 1963 said to Martin:

> People all over the nation have been so aroused . . . that you should call a massive march on Washington to further dramatize the need for legislation to completely integrate the black man into American society. I believe a hundred thousand people would come to the nation's capital at your invitation.

Coretta's idea met with success far beyond her wildest hopes.

Despite the march's success, Coretta was upset that she was not allowed to march with her husband. When she challenged this, the Southern Christian Leadership Conference was adamant that only the men march. She felt strongly that she and the other wives who had worked so hard with their husbands should be allowed to protest as well. She was, however, allowed to sit on the platform behind Martin and was on hand to hear his dramatic speech.

Coretta was also disappointed that she and the other wives had not been invited to meet with President John F. Kennedy afterward. Only the civil rights leaders, like Martin, had been invited to the White House. Despite the disappointments, Coretta took solace in the knowledge that the march had been such a huge success.

Coretta Scott King, *My Life with Martin Luther King, Jr.*, New York: Bantam, 1990, p. 218.

then sang various spirituals and freedom songs. She called the program "The Story of the Struggle from 1955 to 1965."

Coretta describes the format: "I feel that the Freedom Concert was an inspired concept seeking to combine, in dramatic form, art, and experience in a practical, relevant, meaningful way. . . . My background as a performer in music, coupled with my years of experience as a public speaker, gave me a unique means of communicating these experiences in the freedom struggle which I felt was more powerful and effective than either speaking or singing alone could be."[48]

Over the course of the next five years, Coretta gave more than thirty of these concerts in both the United States and Europe. The more than fifty thousand dollars in proceeds from the events was given to the Southern Christian Leadership Conference.

Coretta's Activism

In addition to her freedom concerts, Coretta also began to speak out about other important issues. Since her years at Antioch College, Coretta had been interested in the movement for world peace. While in Atlanta, she joined the Women's International League for Peace and Freedom, a group dedicated to the search for world peace. In 1962 she served as a delegate with the Women's Strike for Peace organization; she was one of fifty American women who attended. The group sent women to the seventeen-nation Disarmament Conference in Geneva, Switzerland, to urge world leaders to sign a nuclear disarmament pact. Coretta was a firm believer that women could make a difference in world decisions. "I was, and still am," she wrote in 1969, "convinced that the women of the world, united without any regard for national or racial divisions, can become a most powerful force for international peace and brotherhood."[49]

Coretta also spoke out against the war in Vietnam, even before her husband did, by participating in an antiwar rally at Madison Square Garden in New York City in 1965. She also spoke to fifty thousand antiwar protesters in San Francisco in 1967. Her hope was to somehow combine the peace movement with the quest

Coretta, center, stands amid a crowd of protestors at the main gate of the White House in May 1967, one of many events at which she publicly denounced the Vietnam War.

for civil rights. Martin ultimately joined his wife in her stance against the war in 1967. Both were criticized severely by others in the civil rights movement, primarily because of the fear that their participation in the antiwar protests would be a distraction from the fight for equality.

In addition, while her husband was at speaking engagements throughout the country, Coretta added her voice to his by joining other representatives in Atlanta to discuss the desegregation of Atlanta's public schools. She also delivered speeches when Martin was not available. The King Center elaborates on Coretta's involvement: "From the earliest days, she balanced mothering and movement work, speaking before church, civic, college, fraternal, and peace groups."[50]

The Kennedy Connection

In addition to the concerts and her social activism, Coretta also became involved in another issue that closely affected her family. During the years that he led the civil rights movement, Martin was jailed frequently, usually as a result of some march or protest he was leading. It fell to Coretta to explain this to the children. Once when Yoki came home from school crying, she asked her mother why her father was in jail. Coretta explained that her father was a brave man who went to jail to help other people. This explanation seemed to satisfy the youngster who, the following day, informed her classmates that her Daddy had not done anything wrong but was merely trying to help other people improve their lives.

Two of Martin's arrests are particularly noteworthy for the active role that Coretta played in getting him released from jail. In doing so, she received help from an unlikely source. The first instance occurred in early 1960 when Martin was arrested for protesting in a white lunchroom. While he was in jail, the authorities found an old suspended sentence on a minor traffic violation. The judge sentenced him to six months of hard labor at a tough state prison, not a particularly unusual sentence for a black man in the South. Coretta, who was five months pregnant at the time, appealed to the press for help.

Help came from Senator John F. Kennedy who, at the time, was campaigning against Vice President Richard Nixon for president

Coretta takes a call from President John F. Kennedy to discuss Martin's welfare during his time in a Birmingham, Alabama, jail in April 1963.

of the United States. On October 26, 1960, just a few days before the presidential election, Kennedy placed a call to Coretta and said: "I'm thinking about you and your husband and I know this must be very difficult for you. If there's anything I can do to be of help, I want you to please feel free to call on me."[51] Kennedy had previously met Martin in June 1960 and talked with the civil rights leader about equality for blacks. Coretta explained what had happened and asked for help.

Kennedy then asked his brother Robert to intervene. A phone call to a Georgia judge resulted in Martin's release the following day. Martin's father, Reverend Martin Luther King Sr., was so thankful for Kennedy's help that he told his congregation they should vote for Kennedy. A few days later, John F. Kennedy was elected president, thanks in large part to the black voters of the South.

Kennedy would again intervene a few years later, in 1963. This time, Martin was arrested and denied the use of the telephone. After several days without any word from her husband, Coretta phoned the White House and talked to Press Secretary Pierre Salinger. President Kennedy himself was at the bedside of his ailing father, but his brother Robert called and told Coretta that he would pass on her message to the president and would find out what the situation was in Alabama where Martin was imprisoned.

The following day, Coretta received a call from the president himself. He told Coretta that he had sent the Federal Bureau of Investigation (FBI) to monitor the situation and that they had reported that Martin was well. Kennedy added that she should be hearing from her husband shortly. Martin called her fifteen minutes later.

Facing the Danger

Because of the calls and the help they received from Kennedy, both Martin and Coretta felt especially close to the president and the entire Kennedy family. They were both shocked, as was the nation, when President Kennedy was assassinated a few months later on November 22, 1963. Martin turned to his wife and told her that he feared that he, too, would come to the same end. Deep in her heart, Coretta believed he was right.

FBI Harassment

As the civil rights movement gained momentum in the 1960s, the Kings came under close scrutiny by the U.S. government. Director J. Edgar Hoover of the Federal Bureau of Investigation (FBI), in particular, focused on Martin Luther King Jr. Hoover apparently wanted to undermine Martin's support because he believed that Martin was a bad influence on African Americans and was generating far too much power. Hoover also claimed that Martin was a communist.

In October 1963, Hoover, with the approval of Attorney General Robert Kennedy, signed an order to wiretap all of Martin's phones, including the motel rooms where he stayed. Kennedy, who had earlier helped Martin get out of jail, was persuaded by Hoover that Martin posed a possible risk to the safety of the country. The wiretappings were used to discredit Martin. The purpose of the wiretaps was twofold: The director of the FBI, J. Edgar Hoover, believed Martin to be a communist; thus the wiretaps were done to denote any Communist leanings and, in the process, weaken Martin's leadership. They were also used to tarnish Martin's image with both his wife and the public. The FBI sent the reports and tapes to Coretta, alleging that Martin was engaging in extramarital love affairs.

Coretta never commented on the alleged affairs, while the charges of communism were proven false.

Coretta regarded what the FBI was doing as harassment. The move to discredit Martin never caused the couple to part, although it did lead to confrontations between Coretta and Martin. Coretta never publicly acknowledged whether the reports were factual or false.

In addition to this harassment, the FBI also failed to warn Martin when threats against Martin's life were received by the FBI. The possibility of an attack in Memphis was also kept from Martin.

Coretta and Martin did what they could to reduce the danger by never flying on the same airplane. They did this to ensure that their children would have a surviving parent should something happen to one of the planes. Martin also traveled with a large contingent of supporters and bodyguards. Despite these precautions, both knew that if an assassin was determined to do harm, there was little that anyone could do to prevent it. Andrew Young, one of Martin's closest supporters, stated: "Before he was thirty years old, he knew that his death was imminent, and that he would probably not live to 40."[52]

Neither Martin nor Coretta, however, dwelled on their fear. In his autobiography, Martin credited his wife with helping him endure the tensions that surrounded his activism. He wrote: "In the darkest moments, she always brought the light of hope. I am convinced that if I had not had a wife with the fortitude, strength and calmness of Corrie, I could not have withstood the ordeals and tensions surrounding the movement."[53]

Coretta, far right, smiles proudly as Martin is congratulated by members of Norway's royal family after being awarded the Nobel Peace Prize in December 1964.

The Nobel Peace Prize

During these days of danger and constant activity, the Kings received some exciting news that made all their hard work worthwhile. In 1964 Martin was notified that he was the recipient of the Nobel Peace Prize, an award given to a those who promote world peace. The Nobel Committee stated that Martin had been given the award because he had used peaceful means to bring about social peace and social change in the United States. Andrew Young, a longtime friend of both Kings, describes what the award meant to them: "Perhaps his and Coretta's happiest moment came when Coretta received word from the Associated Press and the Nobel Committee that Martin Luther King, Jr. had won the Nobel Peace Prize in 1964."[54] At thirty-three years of age, Martin became the youngest person ever to win the award.

Coretta stood proudly by her husband's side when he was presented the award in Oslo, Norway. In many ways, the Kings felt that the prize had been awarded for something—social equality—not yet achieved. In his acceptance speech, Martin pledged to work even harder to achieve the goal of equal rights for all people. The couple decided to donate the all the prize money, slightly more than fifty thousand dollars, to the Southern Christian Leadership Conference.

Upon arriving home in Atlanta, the Kings were honored with a tribute and testimonial banquet. Around fifteen hundred people, both black and white, attended the celebration. At the end of the evening, the attendees stood, joined hands, and sang, "We Shall Overcome." "We felt, for that night at least," Coretta stated, "it was really black and white together in Atlanta."[55]

Chicago and the War on Poverty

After winning the Nobel Peace Prize, Martin continued to speak out against discrimination and racism with even more determination. In 1966, with Coretta's full support, he initiated "War against Poverty," a campaign to get better housing and jobs for all poor people. He decided to focus on the housing discrimi-

Coretta, left, and Martin tend to repairs in a rundown Chicago apartment building in February 1966 during their campaign to expose the dangerous and unhealthy living conditions of poor African American families.

nation found in the North, where poor blacks were not only unemployed but relegated to slum housing. His campaign took him to Chicago.

Coretta and the children joined Martin in Chicago. They lived in a rundown building in the slums in order to show everyone how the millions of poor African Americans lived. They both wanted the newspapers and other media to cover the extreme poverty that characterized the lives of numerous blacks through-out the country.

The entire family was appalled at the bare dirt floors and the overpowering smell of urine that permeated the entire building. Their furnace did not work, nor did the refrigerator. Coretta and Martin both felt that the experience was very meaningful, especially for their children who had never before witnessed such poverty.

After living in Chicago for some time, all six Kings marched in protest against poverty and the discrimination of Chicago's segregated neighborhoods. It was the first time the entire family had marched together. While the march was successful in that it brought the nation's attention to the poverty and segregation blacks faced in the North, there was no appreciable change in Chicago law or the conditions for blacks in that city.

Memphis

Following the limited success in Chicago, the Kings returned to Atlanta. Martin continued leading the fight for equality in venues across the South. In April 1968 he traveled to Memphis, Tennessee, to support black garbage collectors who had gone on strike and were asking for better wages. This was part of Martin's ongoing War on Poverty.

His trip happened to coincide with Easter weekend. On Thursday, April 4, 1968, Coretta took her daughter Yoki shopping for a new Easter dress. Shortly after they got home, she received a phone call from Jesse Jackson, a supporter and assistant of Martin's and a man who would later become a well-known minister and presidential candidate, from Memphis. He informed Coretta that Martin had just been shot. It was the call Coretta had been dreading and yet expecting for most of her married life. Jackson told her that Martin had been transported to the hospital and that she should rush to Memphis.

Jackson, however, had been less than honest with Coretta, hoping to spare her, at least for a while, the tragic news that Martin had died. He had been shot while he was standing on the balcony of the Lorraine Motel. He and his entourage were there talking about the upcoming march in Memphis when a single gunshot, fired by assassin James Earl Ray, hit Martin. The bullet entered Martin's jaw and traveled through his neck, severing his spinal cord. The wound was fatal.

Coretta received official word of his death at the Atlanta airport where she was getting ready to board a plane for Memphis. Atlanta mayor Ivan Allen took the message for her at the airport and then told Coretta that her husband had died. Rather than fly to Memphis that evening, she opted to return home so she could somehow tell her children that their father had been killed.

At the time of their father's death, Yoki was twelve, Martin was

Coretta, wearing a black mourning veil, takes her husband's place to lead a march in Memphis, Tennessee, on the day before Martin's funeral in April 1968.

ten, Dexter was seven, and Bernice was five. The children learned of their father's death from the news on television before their mother arrived back home. Dexter later talked about his mother coming home that night: "Pain filled Mother's face. She encircled us . . . in her arms and drew in a deep breath. . . . Mother had dreaded coming back to the house. . . . How do you tell a child . . . that their father is not only dead but has been murdered?"[56] When Yoki later asked Coretta whether she should hate the assassin, Coretta responded: "No, darling, your daddy wouldn't want you to do that."[57] Coretta remained strong throughout the hours following the assassination, often hiding her own feelings to spare her children.

Assassination Aftermath

In the days after Martin's death, Coretta was extremely busy caring for the children and making preparations for his funeral. On the day before her husband's funeral, however, Coretta flew to Memphis to participate in the march that Martin had intended to lead. Her three oldest children marched with her. Her appearance in Memphis showed the world that she was determined to continue in her husband's footsteps and spread his message. She told reporters: "I am more determined than ever that my husband's dream will become a reality."[58]

Years later, former president Bill Clinton spoke of Coretta's decision to go to Memphis: "We would all have forgiven her, even honored her if she said, 'I'm going home and raising my kids' but instead she went to Memphis—the scene of the worst nightmare of her life—and led that march for those poor hardworking garbage workers."[59]

In addition to marching in Memphis, Coretta also planned her husband's funeral, carefully making sure that it reflected the kind of life he had led. She wanted it to pay homage to his spiritual strength and moral courage. After a moving service at Ebenezer Baptist Church, that included a tape of one of Martin's sermons during which he had spoken about his own death and funeral, Coretta led thousands of mourners on foot to Morehouse College for the final part of the funeral. Martin's casket was placed on an old farm wagon and drawn by two mules to the church. Coretta's choice of the wagon and mules was a symbol of the plight of the poor who her husband had worked so hard to help.

Coretta Scott King buried her husband in Atlanta, Georgia, on April 9, 1968. The inscription on his crypt reflects some of the words he once spoke from the steps of the Lincoln Memorial: "Free at last, free at last, thank God Almighty, I'm free at last!"[60]

Chapter 5

Continuing the Fight

During and after the funeral service for her husband, Coretta Scott King displayed the kind of courage that the nation had witnessed from Jacqueline Kennedy after President Kennedy's assassination in 1963. *New York Times* journalist Peter Applebome elaborates: "To the end, Mrs. King remained a beloved figure, often compared to Jacqueline Kennedy Onassis as a woman who overcame tragedy, held her family together, and became an inspirational presence around the world."[61]

Unlike Kennedy who sought privacy and avoided the limelight, King had no intention of being a silent widow. She pledged to continue her husband's work and, throughout the remainder of her life, spoke out against racism and other issues. She, like her husband, had great charisma and used this to her advantage to implement her own dreams.

In addition to remaining active in the fight for equal rights, she also continued her contributions to Ebenezer Baptist Church where she sang in the choir and served on various church committees. Over time, she received honorary doctorates from more than sixty universities; wrote three books, as well as a nationally syndicated column for the *New York Times*; and was a participant in many historic moments. She usually credited her deep religious faith for helping her to keep going.

Until her stroke in 2005, King worked long hours, gave interviews, sat for photography sessions, and studied the news around the world. Journalist Lynn Norment of *Ebony* magazine spent a day with King and wrote: "Whether she is in her office . . . or comfortably situated in her bedroom study, Mrs. King always seems to be working."[62]

Despite her work on various causes after Martin's death King always made her children her first priority. Her children were all under the age of thirteen at the time of their father's death. She devoted herself to providing them with support and encouragement as the entire family struggled to deal with Martin's death. When she did have to travel, she made sure family friends were there to take care of her children. She also provided support to the children as the entire family dealt with the subsequent assassination of Martin's mother while she was playing "The Lord's Prayer" on the piano at Ebenezer Baptist Church. Alberta Williams King was killed on June 30, 1974, by a deranged African American man who claimed he shot her because of his belief that all Christians were evil.

Honoring Commitments

In the year following Martin's death, King received over 250,000 pieces of mail, including numerous invitations for her to speak at various events and venues. She pledged to personally answer as much of the mail as she could and set up an office in the basement of her home. Her sister Edythe came and helped for several years, but eventually King was forced to hire full- and part-time workers to assist her.

King also kept many of Martin's commitments. She pledged to keep up the fight for civil rights and equality, stating: "I'm more determined than ever that my husband's dream will become a reality."[63] Dexter also spoke of his mother's determination: "What my mother decided to do was continue a tradition of what my father was working on before his death because she honestly believed that his principles and teachings addressing the triple evil of poverty, racism, and war could help to heal America and the world."[64]

Thousands of antiwar protestors gather at a rally in New York City's Central Park to hear an address by Coretta less than a month after Martin's death in April 1968.

King attended an antiwar rally in New York's Central Park a few weeks after her husband's funeral to protest the alarming rise in American deaths in Vietnam. She used many of Martin's words and advised the crowd not to believe everything the government was telling them. A few days after that, she returned to the site of her husband's assassination and spoke from the same Lorraine Motel balcony where he had been shot. There, she helped launch the Poor People's Campaign, telling the audience that she would support any movement to improve black workers' pay and working conditions.

A month later, in May 1968, she joined the Poor People's Campaign in Washington, D.C. Up to that time, she had given many of Martin's pre-prepared speeches. As she spoke at the Lincoln Memorial on June 19, 1968, however, she used her own words in relating not just Martin's vision but her own, as well. King spoke out against continued racism and called on American women to join the fight against inequality. In her speech, she also pleaded for an end to violence and poverty. Also in June she walked arm in arm with Ralph Abernathy, her late husband's friend and cofounder of the Southern Christian Leadership Conference, to the steps of the Lincoln Memorial in another large rally for the Poor People's Campaign.

In late 1968, King was elected to the Southern Christian Leadership Conference's board of directors but also began to work independently of that organization. She gave more freedom concerts in America and in Europe during the late 1960s and early 1970s. She continued her activism on behalf of civil rights into the 1970s. Her influence grew and, by the end of that decade, many candidates for state and national office began to seek out her endorsement of their candidacy.

Hopes for the Future

In the early twenty-first century, Coretta Scott King spoke to an audience at Jesuit University in California and outlined her hopes for the future:

> As we begin the 21st century, I think it is important that people of every race, religion, and nation join together to develop a shared vision of a world united in justice, peace, and harmony.
>
> We should dare to dream of a world where no child lives in fear of war or suffers the ravages of militarism. Instead of spending more than two billion dollars a day on the arms race, as the governments of the world do now, we must invest in human and economic development so that no one has to live in poverty.. . . Let's dare to dream of a Beloved Community where starvation, famine, hunger, and malnutrition will not be tolerated because the civilized community of nations won't allow it.

Coretta Scott King, "Coretta Scott King Reflects on Working Toward Peace," Architects of Peace, http://scu.edu/ethics/architects-of-peace/King/essay.html.

The King Center

In addition to her ongoing commitment to the civil rights movement, King also dedicated herself to preserving her husband's memory and work. She began in the basement of her home where she had, throughout the years, saved Martin's speeches, tapes of his sermons, his clothing, and other memorabilia, including shoes that were still muddy from marching. Dexter spoke of her reasons for wanting to find a way to celebrate Martin's work: "Mother . . . had her own dream. In the aftermath of my father's assassination, she gave birth again, this time to the idea of creating a memorial to my father."[65]

King conceived of a series of buildings to commemorate her husband's work and the ideals which he advocated. The ensuing King Center was built in phases in Atlanta, Georgia, near Ebenezer Baptist Church. She formed an executive board of directors that included former vice president Hubert Humphrey, Senator Edward Kennedy, and Ralph Abernathy. To solicit funding for such a massive undertaking, King and others traveled throughout the country asking for donations. They raised over 10 million dollars.

Dexter King later commented on the project: "We [the children] watched it all come up out of nothing—the reflecting pool and an arched, covered walkway, known as Freedom Walkway. . . . The construction of the center was rewarding to Mother, because it was insurance that her husband's message and spirit would endure."[66] King wanted, according to public radio's Kathy Lohr, "the Center . . . [to become] deeply involved with issues that she said bred violence—hunger, unemployment, voting rights, and racism."[67]

The Freedom Hall Complex of the King Center opened officially on January 15, 1982. It became the first institution in the United States built in memory of an African American leader. The King Center now includes Martin's tomb, his boyhood home, and Ebenezer Baptist Church in addition to numerous buildings devoted to his memorabilia and conference centers, where the fight for nonviolent solutions to social issues continues. By 1990 the center had a 3-million-dollar budget, employed over sixty people, and was attracting over a million visitors each year.

One of the most successful parts of the King Center is its Institute on Nonviolence. This institute sponsors workshops dedicated to teaching nonviolent resolution of conflicts to a variety of groups, including Los Angeles gang members, activists of all kinds, and ordinary community groups. Journalist Heather Gray elaborates:

> The Center was a mecca for civil rights leaders and grassroots activists from all over the world. Youth around the country came to the Center to be trained in nonviolent methods of social change and to meet and be mentored by civil rights' giants . . . there were forums on every conceivable issue of relevance . . . if it concerned a struggle for justice. . . . Of course, her [Coretta] primary interest was to address the triple evils of racism, militarism, and imperialism.[68]

Much of the center today is in disrepair and approximately 11 million dollars in debt. The King Center is a massive undertaking of time and finances. There is also a wide division among the King children as to its future. Some of the children want to turn it over to the government to their time and financial commitment, while other members hope to maintain the Center without government interference in the goals and outlook Coretta envisioned. The children differ in their views about the King Center's future, but remain united in their own fight for equality and the efforts to pay homage to their parents.

A National Holiday

Another of the goals that Coretta Scott King set in the months following her husband's assassination was the creation of a national holiday to celebrate his life. King lobbied for and actively campaigned for such a holiday for nearly fifteen years. Norment summarizes: "Year after year, Mrs. King lobbied presidents, cabinet officials and members of Congress. She also got assistance from other national leaders and entertainers and took her campaign to the people."[69] King testified before Congress and initiated a petition drive that included over 6 million signatures. She and singer

Coretta partnered with singer Stevie Wonder, left, in 1982 to present House Speaker Tip O'Neill, right, with a petition calling for the creation of a national holiday to honor Martin Luther King Jr. The following year, President Ronald Reagan signed the bill that made the holiday official.

Stevie Wonder subsequently took the petition to then Speaker of the House Tip O'Neill for presentation to Congress. Not long thereafter, both houses of Congress finally approved the plan to create the holiday.

King's goal for a national holiday was finally achieved. She was present at the White House on November 2, 1983, when President Ronald Reagan signed the bill making the holiday official. Afterward, she spoke to the 350 gathered guests, stating that the day was a dream come true for herself and her children.

Martin Luther King Day was first observed three years later on January 20, 1986. The three-year delay was caused by the difficulty in getting all fifty states to agree to honor the holiday; this was particularly true in the South. Mrs. King later described

Second Thoughts on the Assassination

In the late 1990s, Coretta and her children tried to reopen the case against James Earl Ray, the man who had been imprisoned for assassinating Martin. Ray, after an initial confession, later claimed he was innocent. Many conspiracy theories about Martin's assassination have also emerged over the years.

Coretta, after a thorough investigation, began to believe that there might have been a conspiracy. She believed there was evidence that Ray had been framed and that the U.S. government may have been involved in the actual assassination. Despite her requests to former attorney general Janet Reno and President Bill Clinton, a new trial was never granted. A limited Justice Department review, however, was done, and after a seven-month investigation, the finding was that Ray had acted alone. Ray died in 1998 before the issue could be resolved to Coretta's satisfaction.

Shortly after the Justice Department review, Coretta filed a suit against Lloyd Jowers, a former restaurant owner, who had claimed that he had taken part in the assassination. Jowers repeatedly told his lawyers and journalists that he had been paid a hundred thousand dollars to plan the assassination. In December 1999, a Tennessee jury ruled that the 1968 assassination had, in fact, been the result of a conspiracy that included the Memphis police and the U.S. government.

Despite the trial verdict, law enforcement officials and historians are nearly united in their belief that James Earl Ray acted alone.

Coretta, center, speaks to reporters in Washington, D.C. in April 1998 after meeting with Attorney General Janet Reno to discuss new evidence of a conspiracy involving her husband's 1968 assassination.

the importance of the holiday: "On this day, we commemorate Dr. King's great dream of a vibrant, multiracial nation united in justice, peace, and reconciliation; a nation that has a place at the table for children of every race and room at the inn for every needy child."[70] Martin's birthday is now celebrated not just in America, but in one hundred other countries.

Many historians consider the creation of this holiday as one of Coretta Scott King's greatest accomplishments. It is the only national holiday that recognizes an American citizen. All other holidays either celebrate a president's birth or a religious or festive occasion. It is also the only holiday celebrating an African American.

The Fight Against Apartheid

In addition to her work on behalf of the King Center and the national holiday, King also took the forefront in the fight against South African apartheid. For generations, the black people of South Africa had been ruled by a ruthless and racist white government. Blacks were forbidden to own property, live in the cities, or hold public office of any kind. They were subjected to even worse discrimination and violence than blacks in the United States had suffered. Poverty, unemployment, and despair were ever present.

Nelson Mandela, a black South African attorney, helped lead a freedom movement during the late 1950s and early 1960s, similar in scope to the civil rights movement led by Martin Luther King Jr. In 1964 Mandela was arrested for his opposition to the white government and sentenced to life in prison. Despite his arrest, he continued to speak out against racism.

Coretta Scott King admired Mandela and, in 1986, traveled to South Africa to lend her support to Mandela's fight against apartheid. Unable to meet Mandela himself, she instead spent time with his wife, Winnie. The two women had much to talk about, sharing the similarities in their husbands' fights for justice, their subsequent arrests, and the difficulties encountered in trying to carry on their spouse's work. King later told reporters that

Coretta traveled to South Africa in 1986 to meet with Winnie Mandela, left, wife of jailed activist Nelson Mandela, and express her support for the fight against apartheid.

she considered the meeting with Winnie Mandela as one of the highlights of her life.

According to Senator Edward Kennedy, King fought apartheid "with the same fervor that she had challenged prejudice in America in the 1960s."[71] In fact, King and three of her children were arrested in 1985 for protesting apartheid in front of the South African embassy in Washington, D.C. Despite her arrest, she refused to stay silent. She returned to South Africa in the early 1990s to witness Mandela's release from prison and the end of apartheid in 1994. She also stood with Mandela when he became the country's first democratically elected president.

An Ongoing Commitment

In addition to standing up against apartheid, King, throughout her life, also continued to speak out against other issues that concerned her. Marian Wright Edelman, founder of the Children's Defense Fund, elaborates: "A strong antiwar and anti-apartheid activist, she spoke to audiences around the world, calling for

Coretta, center, speaks about feminism and the rights of minority women in November 1977 as part of the National Women's Conference, in which she participated at the request of President Jimmy Carter.

racial equality and economic and social justice. . . . Mrs. King was equally passionate about women's rights, and urged women to take their rightful place at the table to create a better nation and world."[72] Because of King's stance, President Jimmy Carter selected her to be a member of the commission for the First National Women's Conference in 1997. The year 1997 had been proclaimed the International Women's Year by the United States. The conference attendees met to identify goals that American women should be addressing in the years to come. It was the only time such a group met. She was also asked to be a public delegate to the United Nation's General Assembly. For her efforts on behalf of this organization, she was awarded the United Nation's Ceres Medal, an award given to honor individuals who work in the campaign against world hunger.

King's campaigns against injustice took her around the world. Shortly after her husband's death, she and her two oldest children went to London. There, she preached at St. Paul's Cathedral, becoming the first woman ever to speak from its pulpit. Later, in a worldwide broadcast, she gave a speech at Westminster Abbey. She also became the first woman to give a graduation speech at Harvard University in Massachusetts. In every speech, she spoke against racism and the discrimination that still existed against blacks and women.

King also addressed the issue of unemployment and, in 1974, founded the Full Employment Action Council. The council's goal was to encourage Congress to enact legislation that would decrease unemployment, especially among African Americans. The council included more than one hundred religious, labor, and civil and women's rights organizations. The organization petitioned for a national policy of full employment and equal economic opportunities. As part of this campaign, King also became a board member of the Southern Rural Action Movement, a group that helped provide people in small towns with better jobs and housing.

King also advocated equal rights for gays and lesbians, the end of the nuclear arms race, and AIDS education. Journalist Zenitha Prince summarizes: "And she fought other battles, traveling throughout the nation and the world in pursuit and in support of racial and economic justice, employment opportunities, gay and lesbian rights, the needs of the poor and homeless, parity in health care, AIDS awareness, and the reduction of gun violence among other concerns."[73] To help with these battles she brought together more than eight hundred different human rights organizations to form the umbrella group, Coalition of Conscience, in 1983. In talking about her involvement, King told Norment: "There is no problem that we can't solve if we can corral our resources behind it."[74]

King was also adamant in her support of gun control, working closely with Sarah and Jim Brady. Brady, former press secretary to President Ronald Reagan, had been severely injured during an attempted assassination of President Reagan in 1981. Together, they petitioned every Congress and each subsequent presidential administration to take a stronger stance against handguns and other weapons. She also spoke out against violence in the media, especially television, and called for tighter regulations in the industry. "In this country, we vigorously regulate the sale of medicine and severely limit the advertising of cigarettes because of their effect on human health," King said in 1994. "But we allow virtually anyone in America to buy a gun and virtually everyone in the nation to see graphic violence."[75] The fight for gun control, along with the effort to curb violence in the media has continued into the early years of the twenty-first century.

A Tribute to a Fallen Heroine

King continued to speak out against injustice until August 2005, when she suffered a stroke that left her unable to speak or walk. A short time later, she was also diagnosed with terminal ovarian cancer. Shortly before her death, she appeared in public. Journalist Vern Smith elaborates: "She electrified the crowd

A host of dignitaries gathered at Coretta's funeral to pay tribute to her life and work. Among the mourners at the service were, from left, President George W. Bush and first lady Laura Bush, former President Bill Clinton and Senator Hillary Clinton, former President George Bush, and former President Jimmy Carter and Rosalynn Carter.

during the King Center's annual Salute to Greatness Dinner at Atlanta's Hyatt Regency Hotel . . . drawing a standing ovation as aides wheeled her into the ballroom."[76] She also made a surprise appearance at a children's program and, while she could not speak to the children, she welcomed them to the King Center with her smile. She died on January 31, 2006, at Santa Monica Health Hospital, an alternative treatment facility in Mexico. She was seventy-eight years old.

Nearly two hundred thousand people waited in long lines at three different public viewings: one at the Georgia Capitol, one at Ebenezer Baptist Church in Atlanta, and one at the New Birth Missionary Church in Lithonia, Georgia, near Atlanta. Coretta Scott King was the first woman and the first African American to lie in state in the Georgia Capitol. At Ebenezer, she lay directly below the pulpit where her husband had preached. Her daughter, Bernice, performed the service at New Birth Missionary Church where she was the pastor. President George W. Bush ordered flags flown at half-staff throughout the nation.

In a six-hour-long funeral service, televised throughout the United States, statesmen, religious leaders, and family honored Coretta Scott King and her legacy to the world. President Bush spoke for many when he said:

> I've come today to offer the sympathy of our entire nation at the passing of a woman who worked to make our nation whole . . . Americans knew her husband only as a young man. We knew Mrs. King in all the seasons of her life—and there was grace and beauty in every season. As a great movement of history took shape, her dignity was a daily rebuke to the pettiness and cruelty of segregation.[77]

Georgia governor Sonny Perdue echoed Bush's words by saying:

> Coretta Scott King was one of the most influential civil rights leaders of our time. While her husband was the public face of the civil rights movement, no person is that successful without strong support at home. She was the anchor on

which he depended . . . Coretta Scott King . . . took a morally courageous stand to end segregation in our Nation and fought for equal treatment for all citizens under the law. Mrs. King was a gracious and kind woman whose calm, measured words rose above the din of political rhetoric.[78]

Just as important, however, were the tens of thousands of ordinary Americans who waited in long lines to honor King. Wendy Pearson, for instance, drove to Atlanta from St. Petersburg, Florida, with her three sons, ages ten through fourteen, telling reporters that she wanted her sons to really understand what African Americans had been through.

Legacy

Coretta Scott King left the world with a legacy of hard work and a fierce determination to carry forth the notion of equality in all aspects of human life. Until the very end of her life, she fought against prejudice and discrimination and never hesitated to speak out against those who sought to deny any people their civil and human rights. In 2006 House of Representatives Majority Leader Nancy Pelosi of California said: "In the nearly forty years (since Martin Luther King, Jr.'s death), she agitated, she struggled, and she remained committed to the vision. She was a civil rights leader in her own right, and with her singularity of purpose and sheer tenacity, she often triumphed."[79]

As part of her legacy, she leaves behind her four successful children. She helped her children through the worst of times following their father's death and supported their decisions and careers. Yolanda "Yoki" King became a successful actress and motivational speaker, who at her mother's funeral stated: "Our mother taught us unconditional love by being that herself."[80] Dexter Scott King became a successful writer and filmmaker, while Martin Luther King III became a Fulton county commissioner in Atlanta, and Bernice King became a minister and lawyer.

King's greatest legacies, however, are the national holiday that celebrates her husband's life and the King Center which has con-

From left, Martin Luther King III, Dexter King, Yolanda King, and Bernice King lead a ceremony at the King Center for Nonviolent Social Change in Atlanta, Georgia, in November 2006 to reveal a new crypt dedicated to their parents.

tinued the fight for nonviolent solutions to social problems. Both the holiday and the center remain living proof of Coretta's determination that her husband's dream of equality would survive. Journalist Barbara A. Reynolds elaborates: "Let us celebrate her as she saw herself: a woman of substance, a partner in the dream, a freedom fighter in her own right, who helped institutionalize the memory of Dr. King for all people for generations to come."[81]

Bernice King described her mother at the funeral, stating that she was "a woman of authority, a woman of power, a woman of grace, a woman of essence, a woman of strength, a woman of dignity."[82] Few would disagree. Reverend Jesse Jackson was in Memphis with other close supporters of Dr. King when Martin was killed and he remained a lifelong friend of Coretta. Speaking at her funeral, he said: "I knew Coretta for more than forty years. To observe her handle the highs and lows of life with dignity was a lesson watching someone master fate with faith. She endured pain with unusual strength and character. . . . Her voice for justice at home, and peace in the world remained a constant."[83]

Perhaps Congressman John Lewis summed it up best: "Coretta Scott King was a beautiful person. She was smart, determined and she acted with poise, grace, and dignity. She was a leader, a friend, a citizen of the world. She traveled all over the world . . . preaching a message of hope, love, and peace."[84] She is remembered best for her courage after Martin's death, her continued fight for civil rights, and her persistent struggle for those whose rights were being denied, whether in the United States or abroad.

Notes

Introduction: The First Lady of the Civil Rights Movement

1. Marian Wright Edelman, "Coretta Scott King Shared the Dream," *Philadelphia Tribune*, February 14, 2006.
2. Brian Robinson, "Coretta Scott King: More than Martin's Widow," ABCNews.com, February 7, 2006, www.abcne ws.go.com/print?id=1585596.
3. Ernie Suggs, "Coretta Scott King," *Atlanta Journal-Constitution*, January 31, 2006, www.ajc.com/metro/content/metro/atla nta/stories/0121metkingobit.html. [Accessed December 1, 2007].
4. Quoted in Suggs, "Coretta Scott King."
5. Quoted in Vern E. Smith, "First Lady for Coretta Scott King, a Royal Farewell," *Crisis*, March 1, 2006.

Chapter One: Growing Up with Segregation

6. Quoted in "Coretta Scott King Shared and Continued Dr. King's Dream," *Tri-State Defender*, February 8, 2006.
7. Quoted in Smith, "First Lady for Coretta Scott King."
8. Vicki Crawford, "Coretta Scott King and the Struggle for Civil and Human Rights: An Enduring Legacy," *Journal of African American History*, January 1, 2007.
9. Coretta Scott King, *My Life with Martin Luther King, Jr.* New York: Henry Holt, 1983, p. 18.
10. King, *My Life with Martin Luther King, Jr.*, p. 29.
11. Peter Applebome, "Coretta Scott King, 78, Widow of Dr. Martin Luther King, Jr. Dies," *International Herald Tribune*, February 1, 2006, http://iht.com/articles/2006/01/21/news/king.php.
12. Quoted in Zenitha Prince, "Coretta Scott King, a Leader in Her Own Right," *Baltimore Afro-American*, February 10, 2006.
13. King, *My Life with Martin Luther King, Jr.*, p. 22.
14. King, *My Life with Martin Luther King, Jr.*, p. 23.

15. King, *My Life with Martin Luther King, Jr.*, p. 25.
16. Quoted in Crawford, "Coretta Scott King and the Struggle for Civil and Human Rights."
17. Quoted in Crawford, "Coretta Scott King and the Struggle for Civil and Human Rights."

Chapter Two: Preparing for a Musical Career

18. King, *My Life with Martin Luther King, Jr.*, p. 39.
19. AfricanAmericans.com, "Coretta Scott King," AfricanAmericans.com, www.africanamericans.com/CorettaScottKingBio.htm.
20. King, *My Life with Martin Luther King, Jr.*, p. 42.
21. Crawford, "Coretta Scott King and the Struggle for Civil and Human Rights."
22. AfricanAmericans.com, "Coretta Scott King."
23. Andrew Young. "The Untold Story of Martin Luther King, Jr. and Coretta Scott King," *Ebony*, April 1, 2006.
24. Quoted in "Coretta Scott King Shared and Continued Dr. King's Dream."
25. King, *My Life with Martin Luther King, Jr.*, p. 52.
26. Quoted in "Coretta Scott King Shared and Continued Dr. King's Dream."
27. Quoted in Applebome, "Coretta Scott King, 78, Widow of Dr. Martin Luther King, Jr. Dies."
28. Quoted in Clayborne Carson, ed., *The Autobiography of Martin Luther King, Jr.* New York: Warner, 1998, p. 34.
29. Applebome, "Coretta Scott King, 78, Widow of Dr. Martin Luther King, Jr. Dies."
30. Prince, "Coretta Scott King, a Leader in Her Own Right."

Chapter Three: Montgomery

31. Quoted in Carson, *The Autobiography of Martin Luther King, Jr.*, p. 54.
32. Quoted in Smith, "First Lady for Coretta Scott King, a Royal Farewell."
33. King, *My Life with Martin Luther King, Jr.*, p. 95.

34. King, *My Life with Martin Luther King, Jr.*, p. 102.
35. Quoted in Carson, *The Autobiography of Martin Luther King, Jr.*, p. 54.
36. Quoted in Herb Boyd, *We Shall Overcome*. Naperville, IL: Source Books, 2004, p. 50.
37. Quoted in Henry Hampton and Steve Fayer, *Voices of Freedom*. New York: Bantam, 1990, p. 238.
38. Quoted in Carson, *The Autobiography of Martin Luther King, Jr.*, p. 79.
39. King, *My Life with Martin Luther King, Jr.*, p. 124.
40. Quoted in Neal Conan, "The Life and Legacy of Coretta Scott King," *NPR: Talk of the Nation* [radio program], NPR, January 31, 2006.
41. Quoted in Carson, *The Autobiography of Martin Luther King, Jr.*, p. 37.
42. Quoted in Smith, "First Lady for Coretta Scott King, a Royal Farewell."
43. King, *My Life with Martin Luther King, Jr.*, p. 144.

Chapter Four: Triumph and Tragedy

44. Edelman, "Coretta Scott King Shared the Dream."
45. Dexter Scott King with Ralph Wiley, *Growing up King*. New York: Warner, 2003, p. 9.
46. Quoted in "Coretta Scott King Shared and Continued Dr. King's Dream."
47. Quoted in Carson, *The Autobiography of Martin Luther King, Jr.*, p. 72.
48. King, *My Life with Martin Luther King, Jr.*, p. 75.
49. King, *My Life with Martin Luther King, Jr.*, p. 193.
50. King Center, "Mrs. Coretta Scott King Human Rights Activist and Leader," King Center, www.thekingcenter.org/csk/bio.html.
51. Quoted in Hampton and Fayer, *Voices of Freedom*, p. 69.
52. Young, "The Untold Story of King Luther King, Jr. and Coretta Scott King."
53. Quoted in Carson, *The Autobiography of Martin Luther King, Jr.*, p. 37.

54. Young, "The Untold Story of Martin Luther King, Jr. and Coretta Scott King."

55. King, *My Life with Martin Luther King, Jr.*, p. 16.

56. King with Wiley, *Growing up King*, pp. 48–50.

57. King, *My Life with Martin Luther King, Jr.*, p. 297.

58. Quoted in Conan, "The Life and Legacy of Coretta Scott King."

59. Quoted in "Former President William J. Clinton and U.S. Senator Hillary Clinton Deliver Remarks at Funeral for Coretta Scott King," Political Transcript Wire, February 7, 2006.

60. Quoted in King, *My Life with Martin Luther King, Jr.*, p. 208.

Chapter Five: Continuing the Fight

61. Applebome, "Coretta Scott King, 78, Widow of Dr. Martin Luther King, Jr. Dies."

62. Lynn Norment, "Coretta Scott King: The Woman Behind the King," *Ebony*, January 1, 1990.

63. Quoted in Kathy Lohr, "Coretta Scott King Honored as Civil Rights Champion," NPR, February 7, 2006, www.npr.org/templates/story/story.php?storyID=5180053.

64. King with Wiley, *Growing up King*, p. 62.

65. King with Wiley, *Growing up King*, p. 69.

66. King with Wiley, *Growing up King*, p. 113.

67. Lohr, "Coretta Scott King Honored as Civil Rights Champion."

68. Heather Gray, "Remembering Coretta Scott King, the Untiring Advocate for Justice," *Atlanta Inquirer*, February 18, 2006.

69. Norment, "Coretta Scott King."

70. Quotes by Coretta Scott King, "The Meaning of the Martin Luther King, Jr. Holiday," King Center, www.thekingcenter.org/holiday.

71. Quoted in Clarence Waldron, "Thousands Bid Farewell to Coretta Scott King," *Jet*, February 27, 2006.

72. Edelman, "Coretta Scott King Shared the Dream."

73. Prince, "Coretta Scott King, a Leader in Her Own Right."

74. Quoted in Norment, "Coretta Scott King."

75. Quoted in Lohr, "Coretta Scott King Honored as Civil Rights Champion."
76. Smith, "First Lady for Coretta Scott King, a Royal Farewell."
77. Quoted in Waldron, "Thousands Bid Farewell to Coretta Scott King."
78. Quoted in "Reflections on the Life of Coretta Scott King," *Atlanta Inquirer*, February 11, 2006.
79. Quoted in Larry Copeland, "Queen of Black America Coretta Scott King Dies at 78," *USA Today*, 2006, http://usatod ay.comm/news/nation/2006-01-31-corettascottking_x.htm.
80. Robinson, "Coretta Scott King."
81. Barbara A. Reynolds, "The Real Coretta Scott King," *Washington Post*, February 4, 2006.
82. Quoted in Waldron, "Thousands Bid Farewell to Coretta Scott King."
83. Quoted in "Coretta Scott King Shared and Continued Dr. King's Dream."
84. Quoted in "Reflections on the Life of Coretta Scott King."

Important Dates

April 27, 1927

Coretta Scott King is born in Marion, Alabama.

1945–1951

King attends Antioch College in Ohio, graduating with a degree in elementary education and music.

1951

King enrolls at the New England Conservatory of Music in Boston.

1952

King meets Martin Luther King Jr.

June 18, 1953

Coretta marries Martin.

1954

The Kings move to Montgomery, Alabama.

December 1, 1955

Seamstress Rosa Parks is arrested on a city bus in Montgomery, Alabama.

December 5, 1955

The bus boycott begins in Montgomery, Alabama.

January 30, 1956

The King home is bombed.

1960

The Kings move to Atlanta, Georgia.

1964

Coretta performs her first freedom concert in New York City.

1964

Martin receives the Nobel Peace Prize.

April 4, 1968

Martin is assassinated in Memphis, Tennessee.

January 15, 1982

The King Center opens in Atlanta, Georgia. King is founder and president.

November 2, 1983

President Ronald Reagan signs a bill creating Martin Luther King Day.

1985

King is arrested in Washington, D.C. for protesting apartheid.

January 20, 1986

Martin Luther King Day is celebrated for the first time.

August 2005

King has a stroke and is diagnosed with cancer.

January 31, 2006

Coretta Scott King dies in Mexico.

For More Information

Books

Taylor Branch, *Pillar of Fire: America in the King Years: 1963–1965*. New York: Simon and Schuster, 1998. Pulitzer Prize–winning author focuses on the civil rights movement and King's [Martin] actions during that period of time.

Dale Evva Gelfand, *Coretta Scott King: Civil Rights Activist*. New York: Chelsea House, 2007. An excellent biography of Coretta Scott King.

Stephanie Sammartino McPherson, *Coretta Scott King*. Minneapolis, MN: Twenty-First Century Books, 2008. A solid biography of Coretta Scott King.

Diane McWhorter, *A Dream of Freedom*. New York: Scholastic, 2004. A good look at the civil rights movement.

Diane Patrick, *Coretta Scott King*. New York: Franklin Watts, 1991. A biography of Coretta Scott King.

Lillie Patterson, *Coretta Scott King*. Champaign, IL: Garrard, 1977. A biography that focuses on King's early life and her marriage to Martin Luther King Jr.

Lillie Patterson, *Martin Luther King, Jr. and the Freedom Movement*. New York: Facts On File, 1989. This book looks at Martin Luther King Jr., his marriage, and his and Coretta's involvement in the civil rights struggle.

Anne Scraff, *Coretta Scott King: Striving for Civil Rights*. Springfield, NJ: Enslow, 1997. An excellent biography of Coretta Scott King.

Robert Weisbrot, *Freedom Bound: A History of America's Civil Rights Movement*. New York: Norton, 1990. This book discusses the civil rights movement through the 1970s.

Internet Sources

William Jelani Cobb, "An Appreciation: Coretta Scott King (1927–2006)," *Black Voices*, January 31, 2006, www.blackvoices.com/newsarticle/_a/an-appreciation-coretta-scott-king-1927/20060131100809990001.

"Coretta Scott King," *Boston Globe*, February 1, 2006, www.boston.com/news/globe/editorial_opinion/editorials/articles/2006/02/01/coretta_scott_king.

Greg Fulton, "Coretta Scott King," *Time*, January 31, 2006, www.time.com/time/nation/article/0,8599,1154673,00.html.

Jerrold Smith, "Uncovering the Coverage," *Fair Play* 3, March/April 2000, www.acorn.net/jfkplace/09/fp.back_issues/33rd_Issue/jowers.html.

"Women's History: Coretta Scott King," Gale Cengage Learning, http://gale.com/free_resources/whm/bio/king_c_s.htm.

Newspapers

Mae Gentry, "Coretta Scott King: Center's Sale May Speed Up," *Atlanta Journal-Constitution*, February 2, 2006.

Jeremy Levitt, "Coretta Scott King: A History Maker in Her Own Right," *Chicago Sun-Times*, February 4, 2006.

Joyce Howard Price and Robert Redding Jr. "Coretta Scott King Dies." *Washington Times*, February 1, 2006.

Periodicals

"Michael Bolton to Perform at Coretta Scott King Musical Memorial," *Business Wire*, February 7, 2006.

Myrlie Evers-Williams, "Coretta Scott King: My Friend," *Crisis*, March 1, 2006.

Web Site

The King Center (www.thekingcenter.org). This is the Web site of the King Center, located in Atlanta, Georgia. Founded by Coretta Scott King, the center continues the work of her husband, Martin Luther King Jr. The Web site includes information about the center's programs, the meaning of Martin Luther King Day, and biographies of Coretta and Martin.

St. Paul's Cathedral (London, England), 80
"The Story of the Struggle from 1955 to 1965" (King, Coretta Scott), 55, 57
Stride Toward Freedom (King, Martin Luther, Jr.), 49–50
Suggs, Ernie, 12
Supreme Court decisions, 38, 47

Transportation, 40–47, *41*

Unemployment, 81
United Nations Ceres Medal, 80
Urban League, 32

Vietnam War protests, 27, 57–58, *58*, 72, *72*
Violence
during bus boycott, 43–45
during Coretta's youth, 21–23
in media and gun control and, 81–82

threats against King, Martin Luther, Jr., 61–62

War on Poverty, 63–65, *64*
Westminster Abbey (London, England), 81
Williams, Olive, 24
Women's International League for Peace and Freedom, 57
Women's Strike for Peace, 57
Wonder, Stevie, 76, *76*

Xenia, Ohio, 28

Young, Andrew
on commitment of Coretta and Martin, 38
on Coretta working as a child, 21
on Coretta's courage, 47
on Coretta's music goal, 32
on Martin's feelings about death, 62

Anne Wallace Sharp is the author of the adult book, *Gifts*, a compilation of stories about hospice patients and their caregivers; and several children's books, including *Daring Pirate Women*. She has also written numerous magazine articles for both adults and juveniles. A retired registered nurse, Sharp has a degree in history. Her interests include reading, traveling, and spending time with her grandchildren, Jacob and Nicole. Sharp lives in Beavercreek, Ohio.